THE
CLIMATE
CHANGE
COOK BOOK

HEALTHY RECIPES FOR YOU AND YOUR PLANET

BY PETER TAYLOR | RECIPES BY PETER MOULAM

A NOTE FROM THE AUTHOR

This book contains recipes for healthy and environmentally sustainable meals alongside some hard facts and figures which you may find alarming. Be alarmed! Be alarmed for your children and grandchildren, because they will inherit your action or your inertia. Global warming will not blow over. It will gradually worsen, killing increasing numbers by starvation, drought, flooding, fires, storms, hurricanes and natural disasters. Until it affects us personally, we seem incapable of responding to the world our children will inherit. The future as things stand is not bright for them. So make the changes. Make a difference and start by examining your food choices. Everyone has an immune system which is rather like a military defence system, keeping our bodies safe from external, viral and bacterial attacks. It needs ammunition, which comes from food, so if the food is of poor quality the defences will be poor. A good quality diet will ensure a strong immune system. The suggestions in this book are a guide to the impact you can have on food production, your own health and the health of your planet.

CONTENTS

WHAT IS GLOBAL WARMING?

It's in the news almost every day, but most of us are sometimes confused by the science behind our changing climate. You'll have heard a lot about greenhouse gases; carbon dioxide is the most abundant and persistent of this group, which also includes methane, nitrous oxide and water vapour. These gases are so-called because they create a greenhouse effect, trapping solar energy from the sun's rays by effectively wrapping a blanket around the earth's atmosphere, insulating and consequently increasing the planet's surface temperature.

WHY DOES IT MATTER?

Climate change is a hugely complex issue affecting every aspect of our planet's health, and according to the World Meteorological Organisation (WMO) we have already seen an increase of around 1°c in global average temperatures in the last two centuries. The 20 warmest years on record have all happened in the last 22 years (as of March 2020) which is already leading to rising sea levels, and will contribute to extreme weather events such as floods, droughts, heatwaves and forest fires.

Scientists also predict the rapid extinction of plants and animals – with most saying we are already in the midst of a sixth mass extinction event – as habitats change faster than most species, including humans, can adapt. The knock-on effects for us could range from water shortages to increased deaths from tropical diseases such as malaria, malnutrition, danger to life from the extreme weather events and of course a radical impact on the stability and quality of our food supply. Economically, the effects will eventually be catastrophic.

DOES WHAT WE EAT NOW MAKE ANY DIFFERENCE?

The short answer is yes. Most CO_2 emissions caused by humans are due to burning fossil fuels; plants in general and forests in particular absorb CO_2, so the more CO_2 we pump into the atmosphere, the more forests we need. About one quarter of all greenhouse gas emissions comes from growing food and raising livestock. Recent scientific reports have concluded that avoiding or significantly cutting down on red meat and dairy is one of the most effective ways to reduce your personal carbon footprint. We all need to eat fewer animal products and replace them with plant-based foods, as excessive protein consumption and a deficit of plant-based foods is bad for human health.

There are many reasons for this huge impact, but the main contributors are:

1. The destruction of forests for agriculture, mining and biofuels. This both increases CO_2 emissions and reduces CO_2 absorption.

2. The high levels of methane, which is five times more potent as a greenhouse gas than CO_2, produced by cattle and sheep. Livestock farming also requires huge areas of land and water, often for growing soya or maize which is fed to animals.

3. The fossil fuels required by agriculture for transport, fertilisers and farming equipment.

DO I HAVE TO GO VEGAN?

Luckily for us, The EAT-Lancet Commission produced the first ever scientific report designed to answer this question in 2019 and no, they don't technically recommend going vegan. The report advises that the majority of your diet should consist of mostly fruit and vegetables; then whole grains (such as wheat, oats, rice and barley); plant proteins including lentils, beans and nuts; certain oils and fats like olive oil; and optional small amounts of animal protein including fish, game, meat, eggs and cheese. The commission's aim is to feed a predicted population of 10 billion people by 2050 with a healthy diet that also fits within safe planetary boundaries: in other words, making sure that the food we eat is good for us and for the planet.

The recipes in this book have been created with these guidelines in mind, so you will find a few that feature meat, dairy, eggs and other animal products, although the emphasis is on plant-based foods since these generally have the lowest 'climate footprint' and therefore cause the least damage to our environment. Most studies agree with the general picture shown in the table on the following page.

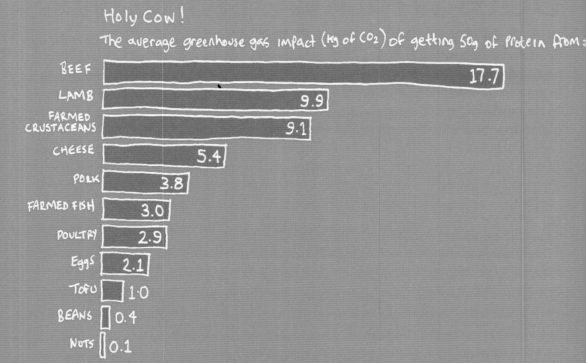

Holy Cow!

The average greenhouse gas impact (kg of CO_2) of getting 50g of Protein from:

BEEF	17.7
LAMB	9.9
FARMED CRUSTACEANS	9.1
CHEESE	5.4
PORK	3.8
FARMED FISH	3.0
POULTRY	2.9
Eggs	2.1
TOFU	1.0
BEANS	0.4
NUTS	0.1

The authors of a recent report discovered that meat, dairy, eggs and commercial inland fish farms use around 83% of the world's farmland, yet only provide around 37% of our protein and just 18% of our calories on a global scale. Protein does not actually provide us with much energy, and because of the various processes usually involved in these kinds of farming, even the lowest-impact animal products tend to exceed the greenhouse gas emissions of plant-based alternatives such as soya.

OK, HOW CAN I HELP?

We can all make a difference, perhaps even more effectively than the producers in our food chain, by choosing to eat food with environmental benefits or at least cutting down on things we know have a big negative impact. The following section breaks down food consumption into five key parts, and suggests a meal plan to help you think about what ends up on our plates in a more environmentally friendly way.

SHOPPING & FOOD WASTE

The Intergovernmental Panel on Climate Change (IPCC) estimates that greenhouse emissions associated with food loss and waste are as high as 8 to 10% globally. From the farmers' fields to your kitchen bin, there's so much we can save or at least compost. We can start by getting organised and learning to use up food that's slightly past its best, such as turning stale bread into breadcrumbs or croutons to freeze for future recipes, and most foods can be rescued with a little creativity. Chapter Nine: Store Cupboard (page 134) can help with this.

It's also important to think about where our food comes from and how it reaches us. The shorter the distance, the less waste created before it reaches your kitchen. Once food has left the farm, emissions can be vast for any product, depending on the materials used to package it and the methods used to transport it. For example, one study found that returnable stainless steel kegs of beer generate the equivalent of 20 grams of CO2 per litre of beer compared to anywhere between 300 and 750 grams from the same amount in recyclable glass bottles.

Other ways to improve your kitchen habits include shopping carefully for planned meals to ensure you're only buying what you actually need, growing some of your own food (even if it's just herbs on a windowsill), using different flours like rye and spelt to support crop rotation, using seasonal gluts to preserve local fruit and veg that you can only buy imported at other times of the year, and buying food with minimal or no packaging. Look for food grown locally – try a radius of 30 miles from your home – and avoid air-imported products where at all possible. It can be tricky to understand all the labelling on our food these days, but there are certain markers of sustainability that can help. They aren't silver bullets (especially as most of these standards are voluntary) but are one way to make more positive choices. In the UK, here are some to look out for:

The LEAF Marque, indicating that food has been produced in an environmentally friendly way by farmers and growers

The Soil Association Organic Standard, from the country's leading organic certifier across a huge range of organic and sustainable certification schemes across food, farming, catering, health and beauty, textiles and forestry

The Marine Stewardship Council (MSC) label, which is only applied to wild fish or seafood from fisheries that have been certified to the MSC Fisheries Standard, a science-based set of requirements for sustainable fishing

Products with the **RSPO Trademark**, available to members of the Roundtable on Sustainable Palm Oil to demonstrate their certification. Palm oil is widely used as an ingredient across the food industry, from margarine to biscuits and ready-made bread to chocolate

The Rainforest Alliance Certified seal, which means that the certified product or ingredient was produced using methods that support the three pillars of sustainability: social, economic, and environmental. This is assessed through the Rainforest Alliance Certification Program and its Sustainable Agriculture Standard

The TerraCycle logo, which denotes a product that may be typically hard to recycle but is part of the company's extensive free recycling programmes around the globe

MEAT

It's often more efficient to grow crops for humans to eat than it is to grow crops for animals to eat before turning those animals into food for humans, especially if land is being cleared to make way for livestock, causing deforestation and releasing greenhouse gases into the atmosphere. However, cows and other livestock can often be raised on pasture unsuitable for growing crops, and they eat crop residues that would 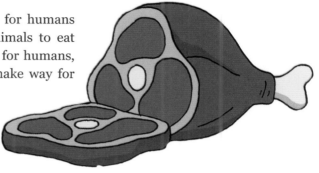 otherwise go to waste. They produce manure that we can use as fertiliser, and animal agriculture provides livelihoods for around 1.3 billion people worldwide.

On the other hand, there are also millions of people around the world — particularly in Europe, the United States, and Australia — who currently eat far more meat than they need to as part of a healthy diet, according to a recent report. Since the goal is to feed a growing population without adding to global warming or putting increased pressure on the world's forests, it would make a difference if the heaviest meat eaters cut back.

The good news for serious meat eaters is that meat production is gradually becoming more sustainable in some areas. There's debate about whether grass-fed beef is better for the environment, but advances in animal breeding, veterinary care, feed quality and grazing systems are already helping to shrink the climate footprint of livestock operations around the world. There's a lot of room for further improvement, so in the meantime, cutting down is the best way to reduce your carbon footprint and benefit your own health by enjoying red meat as an occasional treat rather than an everyday food.

DAIRY

The consensus from scientific studies is that milk typically has a smaller climate footprint than the same quantity of chicken or pork. Yoghurt also falls into this category. However, depending on the variety, cheese can produce more emissions than those same meats because of the amount of milk used to produce it. If you eat a lot of cheese – for example, replacing white meat with cheddar to make vegetarian meals – then your own climate footprint might not have fallen very much. In this case, plant-based alternatives to dairy are a good option.

A 2018 study by researchers at the University of Oxford showed that producing a glass of dairy milk results in almost three times more greenhouse gas emissions and requires nine times more land than any plant-based alternatives such as soya or oat milk, which have little negative impact on the environment unless forests have been cleared for crop production, such as soya which is frequently grown for animal feed. Land is also required to pasture the dairy cows as well as growing their feed, which the animals burp out in the form of methane, a greenhouse gas.

SEAFOOD

Around 60% of the world's fish stocks are currently fully-fished, meaning they're at a sustainable level and the fisheries' potential is being reached. 33% are currently overfished due to unsustainable practices, so there's not a lot of room for huge increases in the amount of fish we consume. However, generally speaking fish is a better choice than most meats, with the exception of poorly managed practices such as the clearing of important habitats to create space for vast commercial fish farms.

Climate change is also threatening marine life as a result of warming seas, and the excessive application of nitrogen and phosphorus fertilisers in food production leading to runoff into streams and rivers. This over-enriches the plants and marine ecosystems with minerals and nutrients, starving fish of their oxygen supply.

As a protein-rich food and a source of essential Omega 3 fatty acids, fish is an important part of our diet. In terms of managing its environmental impact on a personal level, choose fresh fish over processed items like fish fingers because the post-farm impact will be lower.

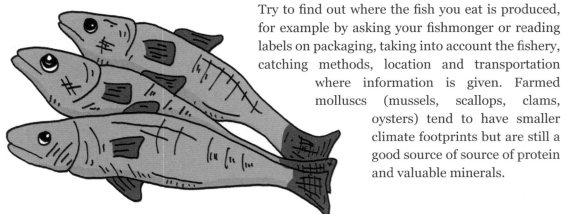

Try to find out where the fish you eat is produced, for example by asking your fishmonger or reading labels on packaging, taking into account the fishery, catching methods, location and transportation where information is given. Farmed molluscs (mussels, scallops, clams, oysters) tend to have smaller climate footprints but are still a good source of source of protein and valuable minerals.

PLANTS

Most science-based approaches to the impact of food production and consumption on climate change agree that a vegan diet has a lower impact on the environment than other diets. Even swapping out some of the animal products in your diet could make a big difference, as shown by the graph below.

It can be cheaper to eat a mostly plant-based diet, and you should be able to find locally grown produce more easily. What you eat matters a lot more than where it comes from, since transportation accounts for only about 6% of food's total climate footprint. However, aiming to make the most of what's in season can be a fun and inspiring way to experiment with vegetarian or vegan cooking. As more and more people embrace this lifestyle change, plant-based alternatives to animal products are far more widely available, affordable and tastier too. However flexible your diet, the majority of your meals should be coming from plant-based sources for your personal health and to reduce your climate footprint most effectively when it comes to what and how we eat.

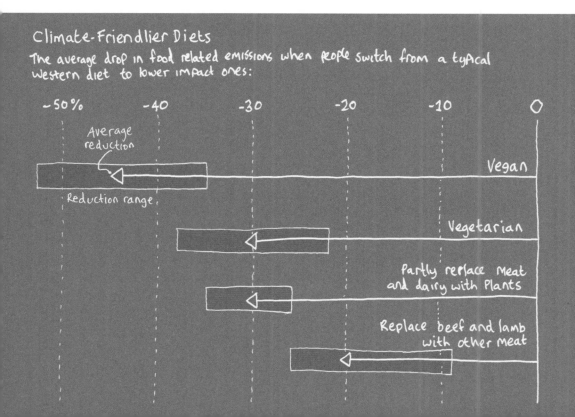

Climate-Friendlier Diets

The average drop in food related emissions when people switch from a typical western diet to lower impact ones:

SUGGESTED WEEKLY MEAL PLAN

BREAKFAST
HOMEMADE MUESLI

50% oats

1 large cup of sultanas

1 large cup of raisins

1 cup of mixed seeds

1 cup of mixed nuts

1 cup of wheat bran

1 cup of wheat germ

1 cup of linseeds

2 cups of psyllium husks

Simply mix all the ingredients together in a large container. Have one bowl daily with plant-based milk, blueberries and the occasional banana. Throw in any other berries you like when they are in season, or use frozen berries for the rest of the year.

This breakfast is full of slow release energy (oats), minerals (nuts and seeds), oil (nuts), vitamins (raisins, sultanas and blueberries), fibre (bran, oats and psyllium husks), nutrients (wheat germ), antioxidants (blueberries) and potassium (bananas).

LUNCH
HOMEMADE SOUPS AND SALADS

Never throw away food; almost any vegetables, beans, pulses and legumes can be used to easily make a great soup. Use leeks or onions as a base and thicken with lentils or potatoes. Keep stock from any meat or poultry dishes and add it to soups for flavour. Try to avoid ready-made stock cubes because they tend to contain large amounts of salt. Aim to become an inventive soup creator by not being afraid to experiment with herbs.

Soups are rich in minerals and fibre but generally contain little to no fat. Carbohydrates like potatoes and lentils will provide energy, and you can serve your soup with a salad or a sandwich for extra nutrients. It's good to avoid heavy meals at lunchtime, especially if you are in the habit of eating a large dinner.

DINNER

You should ideally make a conscious decision to only eat red meat once a week at the most, or give it up altogether apart from special occasions. If you are determined to continue eating meat then be aware that it takes longer to digest and heavy portions of red meat tend to keep people awake if eaten at dinner because of this.

Try to keep evening meals to no more than one course on a daily basis. For habitual meat eaters, try not to exceed the following during a typical week:

Red Meat or Offal   x 1

Fish   x 2

Poultry or Game   x 2

The rest of your meals should be vegetarian, and each meal should be accompanied by three vegetables of your choice plus whole grains like brown rice, or potatoes or salad. Limit your salt and sugar intake by making sauces from scratch and avoiding processed foods.

Here is a suggested plan for healthy and climate-friendly breakfasts, lunches and dinners over a typical week:

MONDAY

Breakfast - Bircher Pot

Lunch - Nettle & Potato Soup

Dinner - Salmon en Papillote

TUESDAY

Breakfast - Strawberry Smoothie with Oats & Chia Seeds

Lunch - Multi Grain & Sprouting Seed Salad

Dinner - Gujarati Style Curry

WEDNESDAY

Breakfast - Homemade Muesli

Lunch - Feta, Chilli & Thyme Scones

Dinner - Millet & Cashew Stir-Fry with Lime & Chilli Sauce

THURSDAY

Breakfast - Blackberry Smoothie with Coconut Milk

Lunch - Butter Bean Bruschetta with Gremolata

Dinner - Tomato & Barley Risotto

FRIDAY

Breakfast - Banana Muffins

Lunch - Roast Vegetable & Smoked Cheese Sourdough Toastie

Dinner - Squash & Bean 'Currito'

SATURDAY

Breakfast - Arepas with Guacamole & Spicy Tomato Salsa

Lunch - Smoked Tofu & Noodle Salad

Dinner - Roast Cod with Shiitake Mushrooms & Miso Broth

SUNDAY

Breakfast - Buckwheat Pancakes

Lunch - Herby Crumbed Chicken Thighs

Dinner - Celeriac & Chestnut Pie with Mushroom Sauce

Create your own meal plans and use all the recipes that follow as inspiration to embrace a more plant-based diet. You might discover new ingredients and flavours that expand your cooking and baking repertoire, and gain a new or deepened awareness of how to eat healthily for yourself and your planet.

CHAPTER ONE: BREAKFAST

BANANA MUFFINS

Next time you have a couple of bananas turning brown in the fruit bowl, don't even think about throwing them out! Make these tasty breakfast treats instead, which have a lovely nutty flavour from the spelt or wholemeal flour.

Prep: 20 mins
Cook: 30 mins
Serves: 10

125g self-raising flour

125g spelt or wholemeal flour

100g caster sugar

2 tsp baking powder

1 tsp bicarbonate of soda

1 tsp mixed spice

2 large ripe bananas

75g butter, melted

2 free-range eggs

125ml milk

To serve

50g banana chips
(see page 138)

200ml yoghurt
or crème fraîche

1 tbsp honey

Preheat the oven to 190°c. Mix the dry ingredients in one bowl and mash the bananas in another. Add the melted butter, eggs and milk to the mashed banana and whisk to combine everything. Make a well in the dry ingredients, then gradually mix in the wet ingredients with a fork. Try not to overwork the flour, otherwise the muffins will be dense and heavy.

Spoon the mixture into 10 paper cases set out in a muffin tray or moulds to support the sides (you can use silicone moulds or individual Yorkshire pudding moulds). If you like, place a banana chip on top of each muffin.

Bake for 20 to 25 minutes in the preheated oven until the muffins are coming away from the sides of the cases. Cool and then serve with the yoghurt or crème fraîche, scattered with the remaining banana chips and drizzled with honey.

BIRCHER POTS

Named after Maximilian Bircher-Benner, a Swiss physician who developed the now-famous muesli as a way of encouraging his patients to eat more fruit. This version is delicious whilst still delivering a brilliantly nutritious boost to start your day.

Prep: 10 mins, plus 8 hours soaking

Cook: 30 mins

Serves: 4 (generously)

50g wheat berries

50g rolled oats

200ml apple juice

2 large apples (a fresh local russet variety is ideal for its nutty flavour)

100ml Greek yoghurt

For layers or toppings

30g roasted hazelnuts or sunflower seeds

Honey

Banana chips (see page 138)

Fresh strawberries or blueberries (when in season)

Soak the wheat berries in water for 8 hours. At the same time, soak the oats in the apple juice for 8 hours or overnight.

Rinse and simmer the wheat berries for 30 minutes until tender and then cool. While the berries are cooking, coarsely grate the apples and combine with the oats.

Stir in the yoghurt and cooled wheat berries. The dish can be served in glass jars using dried or fresh fruit and nuts or seeds to create layers, drizzled with honey if you like. Try the suggestions here or experiment with your own favourite ingredients. You could also use buckwheat, farro or Kamut (all wholegrains) instead of the wheat berries.

BUCKWHEAT PANCAKES

These freeze well and can be reheated for a minute or so in the microwave for an impromptu brunch or lunch. They are delicious served with Cherry Plum Compote (see page 144).

Prep: 10 mins
Cook: 20 mins
Serves: 4 (2 pancakes per person)

150g buckwheat flour
200ml milk
60ml plain yoghurt
2 eggs
¾ tsp bicarbonate of soda
½ tsp baking powder
½ tsp vanilla extract
⅛ tsp salt
1-2 tbsp coconut oil

To serve
Cherry Plum Compote
(see page 144)
Plain yoghurt
Fresh berries

Make a batter by whisking the buckwheat flour with the milk and yoghurt, mixing well to combine everything. Put the eggs, bicarbonate of soda, baking powder, vanilla and salt into another large bowl and whisk them together. Pour the egg mixture into the flour and milk mixture, whisking to make a smooth batter.

Using a large non-stick frying pan, heat some of the coconut oil over a medium-high heat and pour enough batter into the pan to make a pancake about 15cm in diameter.

Small bubbles will form on the surface of the pancake; when you see these and it's firm enough at the edges, flip over and cook for a further 1 to 2 minutes. Repeat to use all the oil and batter.

Serve the pancakes immediately, spooning over the compote and extra yoghurt, perhaps garnishing with some fresh berries if they are in season.

WALNUT & HONEY SODA BREAD

Sweet and savoury at the same time, with an incredible depth of flavour, this is a quick bread which can be made by a reasonably early riser to give friends or family a lovely breakfast. Alternatively, make this to serve with your cheese board.

Prep: 15 mins
Cook: 30-40 mins
Makes 1 loaf

200g walnuts
150g honey
500g wholemeal flour
4 tsp baking powder
10g salt

Preheat the oven to 200°c and lightly oil a baking sheet. Divide the walnuts into two roughly equal piles. Put one half into a food processor or a mortar, then blitz or crush with the pestle to a coarse powder. Using your hands, break the other pile of walnuts into large, rough chunks. Put the honey in a pan with 300ml of water and heat gently until the honey dissolves.

Put the flour, baking powder, salt and all the walnuts into a large bowl and stir to combine. Pour in the honey water and mix to a soft dough.

Turn the dough out onto a lightly floured surface, shape it into a rough, round loaf and place on the oiled baking sheet. Slice a deep cross into the top, going almost right the way through to the baking sheet.

Bake in the preheated oven for 30 to 40 minutes, until well risen and golden brown. Remove, set aside to cool and serve as soon as possible. At the very latest, eat within 24 hours.

BLACKBERRY SMOOTHIE WITH COCONUT MILK

Fresh blackberries are ready to pick or buy from late August to early October in the UK, and they are the tangy, fruity star of the show in this attractive smoothie. Completely vegan, this smoothie can be enjoyed at breakfast time or as a quick on-the-go snack.

Prep: 5 mins

Serves: 2

400g foraged or shop-bought blackberries, washed

200ml coconut milk

5-6 mint leaves

30g desiccated coconut

½ a lemon, juiced

To garnish

2 large mint leaves

2 pinches of desiccated coconut

Place all the smoothie ingredients into a blender and blitz until smooth. Add more coconut milk if you prefer a thinner consistency.

Garnish each glass with a large mint leaf and a pinch of desiccated coconut.

STRAWBERRY SMOOTHIE WITH OATS & CHIA SEEDS

Punchy, colourful and refreshing, this smoothie is a wonderfully nutritious summer breakfast. English strawberries are in season between May and September.

Prep: 5 mins

Serves: 2

50g rolled oats

400g fresh English strawberries

180ml oat milk

180ml apple juice

100g Greek yoghurt

1 tbsp chia seeds

2 tbsp honey

Pour the oats into a blender and blitz until smooth. Add the rest of the ingredients to the blender and process until the mixture is completely smooth.

Top your smoothie with an extra spoonful of Greek yoghurt and a strawberry to garnish if you like.

CHAPTER TWO: BRUNCH

TOMATO & CARAMELISED ONION TART WITH PESTO

This flavoursome tart doubles up as an impressive dinner party starter or rustic lunch. Using beautiful, multi-coloured heritage tomatoes in the summer makes for a real treat.

Prep: 20-25 mins
Cook: 1 hour 15-25 mins
Serves: 2

6 ripe tomatoes (local and grown in season are ideal)

Splash of Henderson's Relish

Salt and pepper, to taste

Sprig of thyme

1-2 cloves of garlic, finely chopped

1 pack of ready-made vegan puff pastry

Soya milk (or other vegan milk)

Caramelised Onions (see page 150)

Handful of pumpkin, sunflower and sesame seeds

Wild Garlic Pesto (see page 152)

Prepare the tomatoes by slicing them onto a baking tray lined with baking parchment. Season with Henderson's Relish, salt and pepper then add the thyme and garlic. Toss everything together then bake in an oven at 170°c for 45 minutes. This draws out some moisture and intensifies the flavour.

While the tomatoes are cooking, roll out the puff pastry to the size of an A4 sheet of paper, approximately 2mm thick. Score a 2cm border right around the outside and brush the whole sheet with soya milk.

Add a thin base layer of the caramelised onions within the border you have made on the pastry base. Next, lay the sliced tomatoes onto the tart. Finally, sprinkle the mixed seeds carefully around the border. Bake in the oven at 180°c for 30 to 40 minutes, checking to achieve a nicely browned pastry edge.

To serve

Let the tart cool slightly and serve with a dollop of wild garlic pesto on top. Great with new potatoes and seasonal salad for a rustic, summery brunch.

BEETROOT & POMEGRANATE TABBOULEH WITH FETA

You can marinate the feta ahead of time, even making double the amount to keep in the fridge for other recipes, as it will keep in the fridge for up to three days. The bright citrus flavours go really well with earthy beetroot and sweet pomegranate.

Prep: 25- 30 mins
Cook: 30 mins
Serves: 4

For the marinated feta
1 orange, zested and juiced
1 lime, zested and juiced
1 lemon, zested and juiced
100ml olive oil
200g feta cheese, diced into 1cm cubes

For the tabbouleh
3 medium beetroot
175g bulgar wheat
1 tsp salt
Small bunch of parsley
Small bunch of mint
50ml Basic Vinaigrette (see page 152)
1 pomegranate
1 x 400g tin of chickpeas, drained

For the marinated feta

Mix the zest and juice of the citrus fruits with the olive oil. Pour this over the cubed feta and marinate for at least 2 hours. It can be kept for up to 3 days in the fridge at this stage.

For the tabbouleh

Meanwhile, either boil the beetroot until tender or rub with oil and seasoning, then roast in the oven at 180°c until tender. Leave to cool, then remove the skins and dice into rough cubes.

Boil 350ml of water and add to a bowl containing the bulgar wheat and salt. Leave for 30 minutes and then fluff up with a fork.

Pulse the herbs in a food processor until finely chopped. Add the beetroot cubes and pulse again until they are in small pieces. Tip the beetroot and herb mixture into the bowl with the bulgar wheat and stir through the vinaigrette.

Slice the pomegranate horizontally in half and hold one half over the bowl. Using a rolling pin or wooden spoon, sharply tap the skin of the pomegranate to knock out the seeds and a little juice, discarding the pith and the skin. Finally, stir the chickpeas into the beetroot tabbouleh and top with the marinated feta to serve.

AREPAS WITH GUACAMOLE & SPICY TOMATO SALSA

Arepas are a South American corn muffin, a great alternative to wheat-based rolls. They work very well with hummus, guacamole, spicy sauces and salsas for a great brunch dish.

Prep: 30 mins

Cook: 20 mins

Serves: 3 (or 6 as a snack)

For the arepas

450ml warm water

Salt, to taste

440g areparina (pre-cooked cornmeal)

1 tbsp coconut oil

For the salsa

3 spring onions

2 red chillies

Small bunch of coriander

160g passata (see page 148)

1 lime, zested and juiced

1 tsp garlic purée

For the filling

2 ripe avocados

2 little gem lettuces

2 salad tomatoes

For the arepas

Preheat the oven to 170°c and have a parchment-lined baking sheet ready. In a large bowl, mix the water and salt together, gradually adding the areparina and mixing until you have a dough that can easily be made into a ball without too much sticking. You may not need all the areparina. Once the dough is the right consistency, cover and leave for 5 minutes.

Separate the dough into equal balls and press out into 1 to 2cm thick discs. Heat a frying pan with the coconut oil in and fry the arepas for 2 minutes or so on each side to form a skin, then transfer them to the lined baking sheet and finish in the preheated oven for 15 minutes. You are aiming to cook the corn cake through to the centre and increase the colour on the outside. They will also puff up and rise a little. Keep the arepas warm while you prepare the fillings.

For the salsa

Finely chop the spring onions, chillies (leaving their seeds in if you like it hotter) and coriander. Mix them with the passata, lime zest and juice, garlic purée and some salt to taste.

For the filling

Prepare the avocados by halving them, removing the stones and skin, then slicing the flesh. Squeeze over a little lime juice to avoid it discolouring. Separate the lettuces into leaves and slice the salad tomatoes thinly.

Slice the arepas horizontally through the middle. You can either completely halve them, which makes filling easier, or not quite slice through to make a pocket for stuffing with the filling. Spread the base with some of the tomato salsa then add the avocado, lettuce leaves and sliced tomatoes to serve.

BUTTER BEAN BRUSCHETTA WITH GREMOLATA

Gremolata is a traditional Mediterranean garnish used to enliven dishes at the last moment. It works beautifully with the creamy butter beans and salty garnish of parmesan and olives.

Prep: 15 mins
Cook: 35 mins
Serves: 4

For the gremolata

1 lemon

½ tsp garlic purée

1 bunch of flat leaf parsley, finely chopped

For the bruschetta

225g dried butter beans or 1 x 400g tin of butter beans

4 thick slices from a sourdough loaf (see page 154)

1 clove of garlic, cut in half

Handful of rocket leaves

4 tbsp olive oil

4 tsp balsamic vinegar

Salt and pepper, to taste

To serve
Hard cheese such as parmesan, grated

Black olives

For the gremolata

Zest the lemon and mix it with the garlic purée, then stir in the finely chopped parsley.

For the bruschetta

If you are using dried butter beans, they should be soaked overnight, drained and then brought to the boil in plenty of water. Simmer until tender, which should take around 30 minutes depending on the age of the beans, then drain and cool under the cold tap. Toss the cooked beans in two tablespoons of the gremolata.

Toast the bread and rub each slice with the cut clove of garlic, then drizzle two tablespoons of the oil over the bread. Dress the rocket with the remaining oil, balsamic vinegar and seasoning then arrange on the toasts.

To serve

Spoon the butter beans on top of the bruschetta, then garnish with the grated cheese and black olives.

HERBY RICOTTA FRITTERS

These are fabulous served with a simple salad of cos lettuce, cherry tomatoes and sprouting seeds (see page 138 for how to grow your own).

Prep: 10 mins
Cook: 5-10 mins
Serves: 4

Small handful of fresh parsley, chives and chervil

3 free-range eggs

250g ricotta

50g plain flour

30g butter, melted

Salt, to taste

Finely chop the parsley, chives and chervil. Separate the eggs, putting the whites in a bowl big enough to whisk them. In another bowl, mix the egg yolks and ricotta cheese together, then stir in the flour, butter, chopped herbs and salt. Whisk the egg whites until fluffy then carefully fold them into the ricotta mixture.

Divide the mixture into six and heat a frying pan with a little butter in. Drop the batter into the pan and fry the fritters on each side for a few minutes, keeping them warm before serving.

Alternatively, make a batch in advance and reheat. They will keep for up to 2 days in the fridge or longer in the freezer.

MULTI GRAIN & SPROUTING SEED SALAD

A highly nutritious salad combining vegetables, grains, sprouted seeds and fresh herbs. As long as you have been sprouting your own seeds, you can make this any time of the year. Sprouted corn, pea shoots, alfalfa and radishes all work well.

Prep: 30 mins, plus 3-5 days for sprouting your seeds

Cook: 30 mins

Serves: 4

700ml vegetable stock

40g wild rice

120g buckwheat

120g quinoa

1 aubergine

4 tbsp olive oil

1 tsp ground cumin

½ tsp ground coriander

Salt and pepper

50ml Basic Vinaigrette (see page 152)

2 carrots, peeled into ribbons

50g sprouted seeds (see page 138)

30g chopped parsley

Bring the stock to a simmer in a pan, add the rice and cook for 5 minutes. Then add the buckwheat to cook for another 5 minutes and finally the quinoa for the last 10 or 12 minutes.

Meanwhile, cut the aubergine horizontally into 4 to 5mm thick slices. Leave them to marinate in a bowl with the olive oil, ground cumin, ground coriander and some seasoning.

Drain the cooked grains and stir the vinaigrette into them along some with salt and pepper while still hot, to allow the flavours to be absorbed.

Using a frying pan or griddle, fry the aubergine slices to tenderise and give them some colour.

To serve the salad, fold the raw carrot ribbons and cooked aubergine slices through the dressed grains. Garnish with the sprouted seeds and chopped parsley.

CHAPTER THREE: SNACKS

ALMOND BUTTER BISCUITS

An excellent vegan biscuit which keeps for a week in an airtight tin. If you can't find almond butter in the shops, it can easily be made at home: see the recipe on page 146 in the Store Cupboard chapter.

Prep: 15 mins
Cook: 15 mins
Makes 20

200g white sugar

100g vegan butter

250g almond butter

1 tsp vanilla extract

190g plain flour

1 tsp bicarbonate of soda

1 tsp baking powder

½ tsp salt

1 tbsp soya milk (if needed)

130g vegan chocolate

1 tsp coconut oil (if needed)

Preheat the oven to 190°c. Add the sugar and vegan butter to the bowl of an electric stand mixer and cream them together. Add the almond butter and vanilla, then mix in. By hand, fold the flour, bicarbonate of soda, baking powder and salt into the wet ingredients.

Try rolling some of the biscuit dough into a ball, and if it's too crumbly to come together add the tablespoon of soya milk and try again.

Roll all the dough into balls and place them onto a parchment-lined baking tray. Aim for around 20 biscuits. Gently press down on the balls with a fork to flatten them. They will expand a little when cooking so leave some space between them on the tray.

Bake the biscuits for 15 minutes in the preheated oven until lightly browned on top. Remove from the oven and leave to cool on the baking tray.

When the biscuits have cooled, melt the chocolate in the microwave by heating for 30 second intervals and stirring every 30 seconds until melted. If your chocolate is a little too thick to drizzle nicely, add the teaspoon of coconut oil to thin it out.

Drizzle the chocolate over the top of the cooled almond biscuits, then leave to set at room temperature before serving or storing.

CAULIFLOWER PAKORAS

Pakoras are a fried snack, usually made with vegetables including potatoes and onions, popular across the Indian subcontinent. They are not unlike bhajis and are a similarly irresistible finger food!

Prep: 10 mins

Cook: 10 mins

Makes 24 bite-size pakoras (enough for 6 people as a starter or side dish)

225g gram (chickpea) flour

2 tsp ground turmeric

1 tsp ground cumin

1 tsp ground coriander

Pinch of salt

350ml almond milk

1 red chilli, finely chopped

1 medium cauliflower, broken into florets

Oil for deep frying

Combine the flour, spices and salt with the almond milk. Stir in the chopped chilli and cauliflower florets, then mix until evenly distributed and coated. Leave the batter to rest for 15 minutes to allow the flavours to develop.

Carefully heat the oil to 180°c in a deep fat fryer or large high-sided pan, then cook tablespoons of the batter in batches, deep frying the pakoras for 5 to 6 minutes until browned. The cauliflower florets should be tender in the centre when they're cooked through.

Drain the pakoras on kitchen paper to absorb excess oil, then serve warm with a traditional Indian-style raita and salad.

CUMIN & THYME POPCORN

Popping your own corn is great fun, quick and very inexpensive. You can experiment with a variety of sweet and savoury flavours. For example, adding smoked paprika and a little dried chilli packs a powerful punch, but the flavours here are more subtle.

Prep: 5 mins
Cook: 10 mins
Makes 1 big bowl to share

2 tbsp olive oil

120g corn kernels

2 tsp ground cumin

1 lemon, zested

Pinch of salt

Small bunch of thyme, leaves picked

Heat one tablespoon of the oil in a pan with a tight-fitting lid. When the oil is medium-hot, test the temperature with a few corn kernels by seeing whether they start to pop within a minute or so.

When it's ready, add all the kernels and ensure the corn is evenly coated with the oil by stirring quickly. Put the lid on and listen for the popping to start while shaking the pan. Keep doing this quite vigorously as everything heats up to ensure the rapidly expanding corn does not force some kernels to stay at the bottom and burn. When all the corn has popped, after about 7 minutes, tip the contents of the pan into a large bowl.

Using the same pan, add the rest of the oil and gently fry the cumin to release its flavour. Take the pan off the heat and mix in the lemon zest, salt and thyme leaves. Stir the flavouring thoroughly through the warm popcorn in the bowl and serve.

KALE CRISPS

This is a great way to use up kale leaves and perhaps introduce people to the divisive vegetable. The fragrant North African spice blend used here is usually a mix of cumin, coriander, ginger, turmeric, cardamom and cinnamon, although there's lots of variations. You could even try blending your own.

Prep: 5 mins
Cook: 20 mins
Serves: 2

100g leafy kale
1 tbsp olive oil
1 heaped tsp ras el hanout

Wash the kale thoroughly, then tear the leaves off the tougher stalks. Dry the leaves by patting them between tea towels. Preheat the oven to 150°c and line a baking tray with parchment.

Tear the kale leaves into bite-size pieces. Drizzle them with the oil and sprinkle with the ras el hanout, then rub the kale with the oil and spice to get an even coating. Spread the leaves out on the lined baking tray and place in the preheated oven to roast for about 20 minutes until crisp but still a nice vibrant green colour. They will actually get a bit crisper as they cool.

Once you've tried these spiced crisps, experiment with different flavourings such as garlic and chilli, lemon and parmesan, or smoked paprika and chilli.

POWER BARS

This nutrient-packed recipe makes an excellent snack which can be cut into portions and eaten on the go for instant energy. Try adding mixed nuts or varying the dried fruits to taste. The chewy caramel texture of homemade banana chips works well compared to hard and brittle shop-bought ones.

Prep: 10 mins

Cook: 25 mins

Makes 12 x 70-80g bars

100g dates

200g prunes

300ml apple juice

300g oats

100g mixed sesame, poppy and pumpkin seeds

100g homemade banana chips (see page 138)

Put the dates, prunes and apple juice into a pan and heat gently to a simmer. Use a stick blender or food processor to purée the mixture, which becomes the glue for the rest of the ingredients.

When the purée has cooled, add the dry ingredients and mix well. Press firmly into a baking tray lined with baking parchment. Place the tray in the oven to cook for 15 minutes at 170°c to set the mixture. Leave to cool in the tray, then turn out and cut into bars. Store at room temperature.

SPELT DIGESTIVES

Rich and delicious, these biscuits are brilliant with cheese or simply as a snack to get you past that mid-afternoon slump without a sugar high.

Prep: 15 mins

Cook: 10 mins

Makes about 35

125g butter

125g spelt flour

125g medium oatmeal

50g soft brown sugar

5g salt

1 tsp baking powder

A splash of milk

In a large bowl, rub the butter into the flour. Stir in the rest of the ingredients to make a slightly sticky dough, adding tiny amounts of milk at a time to get the right consistency.

Form the dough into a disc, dust with flour and rest in the fridge for at least 30 minutes. When you're ready to bake, roll out the chilled dough between two sheets of greaseproof paper until it's an even 4mm thickness all over. Peel off the top sheet of paper.

Press out round biscuits using a 7cm cutter and carefully transfer them to greased and lined baking trays. Bake the digestives for 7 to 8 minutes at 180°c, then leave to cool slightly on the trays before transferring to a wire rack. Cool completely before storing in an airtight container.

SWEET POTATO FALAFEL WITH TAHINI SAUCE

Traditionally, falafels were often made using fava beans instead of or as well as chickpeas. This sweet potato version is baked for a healthier alternative to deep fried falafel. You could mix in some mashed chickpeas or other pulses to experiment with flavours and textures.

Prep: 10-15 mins
Cook: 25-55 mins
Serves: 4

For the tahini sauce

3 tbsp tahini

1 tsp garlic paste

1 lemon, juiced

4-5 tbsp water

Salt and pepper

For the falafel

750g sweet potatoes

1 tbsp olive oil

100g gram (chickpea) flour

2 tsp ground cumin

1 tsp ground coriander

1 lemon, juiced

Small bunch of coriander, finely chopped

For the tahini sauce

Whisk the tahini, garlic and lemon juice together, adding water until you have the consistency that you like. Season to taste with salt and pepper.

For the falafel

Scrub the sweet potatoes under cold running water to clean the skins, then either roast them in the oven at 180°c for 30 to 40 minutes or microwave them on full power for 7 to 8 minutes. Leave to cool slightly before cutting in half and scooping out all the flesh into a bowl.

Grease a baking sheet with the oil and turn the oven temperature up to 200°c. Add all the other ingredients to the sweet potato and mix to combine. Form the mixture into about 20 balls, place them on the oiled tray and bake in the oven for 15 minutes or until they take on a good colour.

Serve the baked falafel with the tahini sauce for dipping, or combine them with some pickled vegetables, chillies, olives and toasted pitta bread for a more substantial snack.

CHAPTER FOUR: LUNCH

ROAST VEGETABLE & SMOKED CHEESE SOURDOUGH TOASTIE

A quick yet tasty and nutritious lunch, particularly if you have reserved some roast vegetables from a meal in the last few days.

Prep: 10 mins

Cook: 5-15 mins

Serves: 1

2 medium-thick slices of sourdough (see page 154)

2 slices of smoked cheddar (approx. 75g)

For the roast vegetables

Mixed seasonal vegetables such as courgettes, aubergines, peppers and red onions

3 cloves of garlic

Olive oil

Salt and pepper

For the roast vegetables

It's handy to have done this the evening before, perhaps as part of a larger batch or while the oven is on for another meal. Dice or slice the vegetables and put them into a roasting tin. Crush the whole garlic cloves and add to the tin along with a drizzle of olive oil and seasoning to taste. Roast in the oven at about 200°c for 30 to 45 minutes, then leave to cool.

To make the sandwich, preheat your sandwich toaster, grill pan or oven. Pile the roast vegetables and any juices from the pan onto the first slice of bread. For an extra garlic hit you can squeeze the softened garlic from the cooked cloves over the vegetables. Cover with a layer of smoked cheddar and add the second slice of bread.

Cook in the sandwich toaster, grill pan or oven until bubbling hot in the centre. Serve sliced in half with a salad, or eaten as a handheld snack in a napkin.

FETA, CHILLI &
THYME SCONES

Spread with Apple Chutney (see page 150) and served warm with a salad on the side, these savoury scones make a lovely summer lunch.

Prep: 15 mins
Cook: 15-20 mins
Serves: 4

350g self-raising flour

1 tbsp baking powder

½ tsp salt

50g butter

1 tbsp olive oil

100g feta, cubed

10 olives, coarsely chopped

1 tsp dried thyme

½ tsp dried chilli flakes

300ml milk

1 egg, beaten with a little milk

Preheat the oven to 200°c. In a large bowl combine the flour, baking powder and salt. Rub in the butter and oil until the mixture resembles breadcrumbs, then add the feta, olives, thyme and chilli. Make a well in the centre and add the milk, using a metal spoon to fold the mixture together into a dough, which should be quite sticky.

Without handling the dough too much, press it gently into a round about 3 or 4cm thick. It can help to use floured hands to stop the dough sticking. Cut into eight wedges or rounds and place onto a parchment-lined baking sheet. Brush the scones with the egg wash to give them a good glaze. Bake for 15 to 20 minutes in the preheated oven until they are well risen and a lovely golden colour on top. Serve warm with accompaniments of your choice.

MACKEREL PÂTÉ & LINSEED CRISPS

Served with linseed crisps and a salad, this makes a light lunch high in Omega 3 oils, essential fatty acids and fibre that's also gluten-free.

Prep: 25 mins
Cook: 20 mins
Serves: 2

For the mackerel pâté

2 whole smoked mackerel fillets

1 tbsp horseradish sauce or 1 tsp freshly grated horseradish root

1 lemon, juiced

2 tsp Dijon mustard

50g unsalted butter, softened

Freshly ground black pepper

For the linseed crisps

100g linseeds or flax seeds

20g potato starch, cornflour or arrowroot (arrowroot gives the crisps a clear finish)

2g salt

For the mackerel pâté

Flake the mackerel fillets into a blender, removing the skin and any remaining bones as you do so. Add the horseradish, lemon juice and mustard to the blender and pulse to make a pâté of your preferred consistency, leaving it as smooth or as coarse as you prefer.

Finally, add the butter and briefly pulse again to incorporate. Check the seasoning; it probably won't need salt but some black pepper makes a nice addition.

For the linseed crisps

Weigh everything out carefully. Mix the seeds, starch and salt in a bowl. Pour 350g of boiling water into the dry ingredients and mix thoroughly. Let it soak for 4 or 5 minutes, until the water has been absorbed enough to create a spreadable consistency.

Pour the mixture onto a baking tray, ideally covered with a silicone mat or good quality baking parchment. It can be useful to invert the baking tray, using the underside so that you have a completely flat surface with no raised edges. Spread the mixture out very thinly and then bake at 160°c for 20 to 30 minutes or until the mixture has dried out and starts to lift off the mat or baking parchment. Leave to cool without removing from the tray.

Once cooled, gently pull the crispy layer from the baking sheet. If you are lucky it will come off in one impressive translucent sheet. If not, break the linseed crisp into pieces anyway ready to eat with your mackerel pâté. These are also good with a cheese board, as a snack with other dips or for garnishing.

QUINOA SALAD WITH ROASTED TOMATOES & HUMMUS

A highly nutritious salad packed with colour and flavour. Quinoa is a seed from a crop originating in South America, and unlike many plant-based foods it contains all the essential amino acids needed by the body to form a complete protein.

Prep: 15 mins

Cook: 20-30 mins

Serves: 4

250g or 2 punnets of cherry tomatoes

300g red, black or mixed quinoa

75ml Basic Vinaigrette (see page 152)

50g black or green pitted olives

1 red pepper, deseeded and diced

½ a cucumber, diced

Small bag of watercress

Mixture of poppy, sesame and sunflower seeds, lightly toasted in a pan

For the hummus

1 x 400g tin of chickpeas, drained with some of the liquid reserved

1 lemon, juiced

1 tbsp tahini

1 tbsp olive oil

1 tsp garlic paste (optional)

Salt and pepper

Put the cherry tomatoes on a parchment-lined baking tray, drizzle them with olive oil and season. Roast in the oven at 200°c for 20 to 30 minutes to soften, add some colour and intensify the flavours and then leave to cool, keeping any juices that are in the tray.

Meanwhile, rinse the quinoa well in a sieve and simmer in boiling water until tender (about 15 to 20 minutes). Drain and cool, stirring the vinaigrette through while the quinoa is still warm so that it can absorb the flavours.

For the hummus

Blend the ingredients together in a food processor or use a stick blender. Adjust the flavour to your liking with more or less lemon juice, olive oil, garlic and seasoning.

Finish the salad by mixing the dressed quinoa with the olives, red pepper, cucumber and watercress. Either arrange on individual plates or use a large serving platter. Create a mound of salad and then a pile of hummus, topped with the roasted tomatoes, dressed with some olive oil and sprinkled with the toasted mixed seeds.

To serve

Serve with good sourdough bread, ciabatta or baguettes on the side.

HERBY CRUMBED CHICKEN THIGHS

These chicken thighs are baked with a flavour-packed breadcrumb coating. Great served with homemade mayonnaise (see page 147) and a green salad.

Prep: 10-15 mins
Cook: 25 mins
Serves: 6

150g breadcrumbs

1 tsp oregano

1 tsp ground cumin

1 tsp smoked paprika

Salt and pepper

75g plain flour

2 eggs, beaten

Splash of milk

12 chicken thighs

6 tbsp mayonnaise, to serve
(see page 147)

Combine the breadcrumbs with the oregano, cumin and smoked paprika, then season with salt and pepper. Preheat the oven to 190°c.

Set up three bowls or trays. Place the flour in one, the beaten eggs whisked with the splash of milk in another, and the breadcrumb mix in the final bowl.

Cover the chicken thighs in flour in the first bowl, then dip them into the egg wash. Lay them into the flavoured breadcrumbs, ensuring the crumb completely covers the chicken in a thick layer. It's easier to do this one by one, using one hand for dry ingredients and the other for the egg.

Bake the chicken thighs in the preheated oven for 25 minutes until golden brown all over and the internal temperature reaches 75°c. Serve with the mayonnaise and a green salad.

SMOKED TOFU & NOODLE SALAD

Have fun with your spiralizer making a really colourful nutrient-packed salad. The tofu adds important protein and carries the marinade flavour really well. For the salad vegetables, you can use the best seasonal combinations including courgettes, carrots, kohlrabi, radishes, spring onions, cucumber, peppers, cabbage or beetroot.

Prep: 10 mins, plus 1 hour marinating

Cook: 10 mins

Serves: 2

For the marinated tofu

1 stick of lemongrass

2 cloves of garlic

Knob of root ginger

1 tbsp brown sugar

1 tbsp fresh lime juice

1 tbsp soy sauce

1 tbsp light olive oil

200g smoked or plain tofu, cubed

For the salad

200g wheat-free noodles

2 carrots

2 courgettes

1 red pepper

½ a cucumber

Small bunch of coriander, chopped

2 red chillies, deseeded and chopped

50g unsalted peanuts, toasted

For the marinated tofu

Trim away the harder green parts of the lemongrass, then finely chop the softer white parts. Peel and crush the garlic and finely slice the ginger. Mix them all together with the brown sugar, lime juice, soy sauce and olive oil, then coat the cubed tofu with the marinade. Leave in the fridge for 1 hour.

For the salad

Cook the noodles in plenty of boiling salted water until tender, then drain and run them under the cold tap before draining again to dry. Use a spiralizer or finely chop the carrots, courgettes, red pepper and cucumber then add to a large bowl along with most of the chopped coriander (leave some for the garnish).

Take the tofu out of the fridge and place it in a sieve over a bowl containing the salad, so that the marinade drains through and acts as a dressing. Add the noodles to the salad and mix well.

To serve

Pile the salad into four largish bowls, top with the marinated tofu cubes and pour over any remaining marinade. Top with the chopped chilli, toasted peanuts and remaining coriander.

NETTLE & POTATO SOUP

The quickest and possibly most nutritious soup you can make: just four ingredients, and one of them foraged from your garden! Nettles have been used for centuries to detoxify the body, boost energy levels after the long winter and improve the nutrient uptake of the gut.

Prep: 10-20 mins

Cook: 20-30 mins

Serves: 2

1 large bowl of nettle tops

1 large potato

30ml olive oil, lard, ghee or butter for a slightly richer flavour

1 chicken or vegetable stock cube

Salt and pepper

First, go out to your garden or local green space to find a patch of young nettles. Pick just the tops until you have enough to fill a bowl. If you have chef's hands you can do this without gloves, otherwise wear sensible PPE!

If you garden without pesticides and other chemicals (highly recommended) these young nettle tops are likely to be highly nutritious, drawing valuable minerals from the soil. In addition, nettles are the host food of the peacock butterfly so by keeping a patch in the garden you can enjoy these amazing, colourful butterflies later in the year.

If you'd rather not use nettles or can't find any, a couple of large leeks would make a good alternative. Slice them thinly and rinse well to remove any dirt between the layers.

After foraging, peel and dice the potato while you heat the fat in a large saucepan. It's best to avoid seed oils which often use a chemical extraction process and contain high levels of Omega 6 rather than the more useful Omega 3.

Add the potatoes and nettles or leeks to the pan and turn to coat them in the fat. Pour in enough water to cover the vegetables and crumble over the stock cube. Simmer for about 20 minutes.

When the potatoes are soft, use a stick blender to blend the mixture into a lovely smooth soup. Season to taste with salt and pepper, then serve hot, or chill and reheat later.

MINT & LEMON CAULIFLOWER RICE

Cauliflower rice is a brilliant low-carbohydrate alternative to rice, and it can be flavoured in a variety of ways. This fragrant lemon and mint version is great with a mild curry.

Prep: 15 mins
Cook: 15 mins
Serves: 4 as a side

70g hazelnuts

500g cauliflower (1 good-sized cauliflower)

1 tbsp olive oil

2 cloves of garlic

4 shallots

2 sticks of celery

1 lemon

30g fresh mint leaves, chopped

Handful of fresh parsley (optional)

Fry the hazelnuts in a dry pan until they have taken on a little colour and released some of their oils, then set aside. Remove the core from the cauliflower and break the florets into a food processor. Pulse carefully so that the raw cauliflower breaks down to resemble grains of rice.

Heat the olive oil in a pan while you peel and finely chop the garlic, shallots and celery. Fry them in the oil for 5 to 6 minutes, then add the cauliflower rice and cook for another 6 minutes.

Leave the mixture to cool a little then zest the lemon over the pan, fold in the chopped mint and scatter over the toasted hazelnuts and some parsley if you like.

Season the cauliflower rice to taste, then serve with your choice of curry.

CHAPTER FIVE:
30 MINUTE MEALS

SALMON EN PAPILLOTE WITH LEMON & DILL

This incredibly simple way to cook salmon ensures you can whip up an Omega 3-rich meal in under half an hour. Serve with a side of green vegetables and baby potatoes for an easy weeknight dinner.

Prep: 5 mins

Cook: 15 mins

Serves: 2

2 skinless salmon fillets (approximately 150-200g)

1 tbsp butter

Salt and pepper, to taste

1 lemon, sliced

Fresh dill, to taste

Preheat the oven to 200°c. Fold a large piece of parchment paper in half, then open up again. Lay the salmon on the top half of the paper. Gently spread the butter over the top of the fillets, then sprinkle with salt and pepper. Lay the lemon slices and sprigs of dill on top of the salmon.

Fold the parchment paper over the salmon, and cinch the paper together on the other side like a large envelope by folding the paper over itself along the edges.

Bake for 10 to 15 minutes in the preheated oven until the fish is just cooked in the centre. You can have a peek and check with a sharp knife in the thickest part to see if the flesh has just turned from its raw translucent state to looking opaque. It's easy to overcook fish and dry it out, but if you catch it at this point the salmon will be soft and succulent.

ROAST SQUASH & PUY LENTILS WITH POMEGRANATE MOLASSES DRESSING

In the UK, squashes are brilliant autumn vegetables with modern cultivars coming in many shapes and sizes. This recipe can be made with any variety except perhaps pumpkins, which because of their watery and bland flavour are best left for Halloween decorations!

Prep: 15 mins (while cooking)

Cook: 30 mins

Serves: 4 as a side or substantial starter

360g Puy lentils

3 cloves of garlic

A couple of bay leaves

A good sprig of rosemary

600ml vegetable stock

2 tbsp olive oil

Salt and pepper, to taste

4 tbsp Basic Vinaigrette (see page 152)

Small bunch of parsley, chopped

1 medium butternut squash

1 red onion

3 sprigs of rosemary

1 punnet of cherry tomatoes

1 bag of baby spinach, washed and dried

½ a bunch of spring onions, finely chopped

1 lemon, cut into wedges

For the dressing

1 tbsp pomegranate molasses

1 tbsp white wine vinegar

6 tbsp olive oil

Put the lentils into a medium-size saucepan with the garlic, bay, rosemary, stock and olive oil. Bring to the boil and cook over a medium heat for about 20 to 25 minutes. Keep an eye on it and add a little more liquid as necessary.

When the lentils are tender, but not mushy, drain them and remove the garlic and herbs. Season with salt and freshly ground pepper, then stir in the vinaigrette and a good handful of chopped parsley. Allow the lentils to cool completely.

Meanwhile, preheat the oven to 190°c. Chop the butternut squash into bite-size chunks, scraping out the seeds and stringy parts. Peel the onion and chop into eighths. Put the butternut squash and red onion into a bowl with a drizzle of olive oil, a pinch of salt and pepper and all the rosemary.

Toss everything together well to coat the vegetables. Pour out into a roasting tray. Cook the squash and onions in the preheated oven for about 30 minutes until soft and just beginning to brown on the cut edges. Leave them to cool and discard the rosemary.

For the dressing

The easiest way to mix this is by putting the pomegranate molasses, white wine vinegar and olive oil into a clean jam jar. Screw the lid on tightly then shake well to emulsify the liquids. Add seasoning to taste.

Combine the lentils, roasted squash and onion, cherry tomatoes and spinach in a bowl then fold through the dressing. Pile the salad into individual bowls or a larger serving bowl then sprinkle with the spring onions and serve with the lemon wedges for squeezing over if you like.

COURGETTE FRITTERS

These wholesome courgette fritters, packed with hidden vegetables, are an easy lunch or a quick but colourful evening meal that children and adults will love. Great for busy weekdays!

Prep: 10 mins

Cook: 20 mins

**Serves: 4
(2 fritters each)**

2 large courgettes

1 small sweet potato

1 large handful of spinach

150g gram (chickpea) flour

1 tbsp ground cumin

Salt and pepper, to taste

200g sweetcorn

2 large handfuls of breadcrumbs

Grate the courgettes and sweet potato into a food processor then add the spinach. Blitz the vegetables for 30 seconds until the mixture is quite smooth.

Add the gram flour, cumin, salt and pepper to the processor then blitz for another 10 seconds. Turn out the mixture into a large bowl and mix in the sweetcorn.

Shape the mixture into 70g balls and press into burger shapes. Dip each one into a large bowl or tray of the breadcrumbs and pat down to cover completely.

Bake the fritters in a preheated oven at 180°c for 20 minutes. Serve with a sour cream dip as a small snack or topped with a poached egg for a more filling meal.

MILLET & CASHEW STIR-FRY WITH LIME & CHILLI SAUCE

Millet is a tasty cereal crop with a fluffy, almost creamy consistency when fully cooked. As well as being a starchy and therefore carbohydrate-dense food, it contains protein and is also a good source of minerals, particularly magnesium which is known to be vital for brain function.

Prep: 10 mins
Cook: 15 mins
Serves: 4

200g uncooked millet

100g cashew nuts

5cm root ginger, finely chopped

4 cloves of garlic, finely chopped

2 large carrots, shredded

200g red or white cabbage, shredded

200g beansprouts

100g spinach or tender kale

½ a bunch of spring onions, finely chopped

For the sauce

1 lime, zested and juiced

2 red chillies, finely chopped (choose the heat level of your choice!)

3 tbsp light soy sauce

3 tbsp honey

Put the millet into a pan and cover with 250ml of water. Turn on the heat and gently simmer until all the water has been absorbed. This should take about 10 minutes.

Meanwhile, toast the cashew nuts in a dry wok or large frying pan until they have taken on a little colour, then cool and roughly chop.

Add some oil to the same pan and lightly cook the ginger and garlic to bring out their flavour. Add the carrots, cabbage, beansprouts and spinach or kale, then stir-fry for about 5 minutes, keeping everything moving by shaking the wok or stirring the contents.

For the sauce, combine the lime zest and juice with the chillies, soy sauce and honey. Once the vegetables are done to your liking, add the cooked millet and mix well, then stir in the sauce for the last 1 or 2 minutes of cooking.

Serve the stir-fry garnished with the spring onions and toasted chopped cashews.

CHAPTER SIX:
SLOW COOKING

ROAST SQUASH TAGINE WITH HOMEMADE HARISSA

A great winter warmer of a dish with its earthy flavours and the heat from the spices. Tagines originate in North Africa and get their name from the earthenware pot in which they are cooked. Serving the harissa on the side allows your guests to vary the final heat level.

Prep: 15 mins
Cook: 45 mins
Serves: 6

For the harissa

80g fresh red chillies

50g roasted red peppers

30ml red wine vinegar

25g tomato purée

4 cloves of garlic, peeled

1 tsp each of ground coriander and cumin

½ tsp ground black mustard seeds

For the tagine

300g squash

300g mixed bell peppers

150g carrots

4 or 5 whole cloves

2 tsp cumin seeds

1 tsp coriander seeds

1 cinnamon stick

100g dried apricots

250ml vegetable stock

2 onions, peeled and diced

2 tsp minced root ginger

4 cloves of garlic, grated

2 tsp ground turmeric

1 tsp dried chilli flakes or 3-4 whole chillies

1 lemon, zested and juiced

400g tin of chopped tomatoes

150g cooked chickpeas

For the harissa

Remove the stalks of the chillies and slice horizontally to scrape out the seeds. Then, simply blend the chillies in the food processor with the remaining ingredients as well as a pinch of sea salt until smooth.

For the tagine

Peel and dice the squash, peppers and carrots then roast them in the oven at 180°c with a drizzle of olive oil and some seasoning. Toast the cloves, cumin, coriander and cinnamon stick in a hot, dry pan to release the natural oils then blitz in a spice grinder or pestle and mortar.

Soak the apricots in some of the warmed stock. Soften the onion, ginger and garlic in a pan for 5 minutes before adding the toasted and ground spices (if using whole chillies, add them here, removing the seeds for less heat according to your preference). Cook for another couple of minutes, then add the stock, apricots, lemon zest and juice, tomatoes and chickpeas, scraping the bottom of the pan to include all the flavour.

Stir the roasted vegetables into the tagine, taste and season with salt and pepper. Simmer for a few minutes to reduce the amount of liquid, but if it gets too dry just add a splash of water. For more sauce, you can use more stock and then thicken to taste with cornflour.

Once done, the tagine can be covered and chilled for later reheating, or served straight away with some fluffy couscous and the homemade harissa on the side. Scatter some fresh coriander and mint, pomegranate seeds and preserved lemon over the top to garnish. For presentation, a traditional tagine dish is ideal but it tastes just as good from a plate!

SQUASH & BEAN 'CURRITO'

A fun fusion of flavoursome cuisines, this curried burrito or 'currito' is a perfect weekend meal full of nutritious beans and vegetables.

Prep: 20 mins
Cook: 1 hour 5 mins
Serves: 4

For the curry

½ a red onion, chopped

2 cloves of garlic, chopped

1 tsp each of garam masala, ground cumin and curry powder

½ tsp each of ground turmeric and paprika

2 carrots, diced

¹/₃ of a butternut squash, diced

1 red chilli, finely chopped

1 x 400g tin of chopped tomatoes

250ml vegetable stock

Pinch of brown sugar

1 x 400g tin of mixed white and pinto beans

Handful of fresh parsley and coriander, chopped

For the rice

100g basmati rice

½ tbsp each of ground turmeric and paprika

For the spicy slaw

50g each of carrot and red cabbage, grated

2 pickled chillies, chopped

1 tbsp apple cider vinegar

To assemble

4 x 25cm tortilla wraps

For the curry

Sauté the onion and garlic in olive oil until softened. Meanwhile, toast the spices in a hot oven or a dry skillet then add them to the pan. Stir in the carrots, squash and chilli, cook for 2 minutes, then pour in the chopped tomatoes and vegetable stock. Simmer for 10 minutes.

Taste the sauce then add salt, pepper and brown sugar to balance the flavour. Turn down the heat and add the beans. Cook until softened slightly. Finally, remove the pan from the heat, fold in the chopped fresh herbs and leave to cool.

For the rice

Boil the rice in a large pan of salted water until cooked (this should take approximately 8 minutes). Remove from the heat and drain off the hot water. Cool by placing the pan containing the rice under the cold tap for a few minutes before draining thoroughly again. When cooled and drained, stir in the spices.

For the spicy slaw

Add all the ingredients to a bowl, stir to combine everything and leave to marinate for 30 minutes while the curry is cooling.

To assemble

Lay out the tortillas then fill each one with rice, curry and spicy slaw in that order. Roll them into burritos by tucking in the ends, wrap individually in baking paper or foil, then place in a roasting tin. Bake the curritos in the oven at 180°c for 30 minutes, then serve hot.

SHIN OF BEEF WITH ALE & DUMPLINGS

Beef shin is muscle meat which comes from the upper part of the front leg of the animal. It contains a lot of connective tissue but long, slow cooking breaks this down to create a delicious sauce, with the gelatine helping to thicken the gravy. A lovely winter dish.

Prep: 15 mins

Cook: approx. 1 hour 45 mins

Serves: 2

For the beef stew

1 onion, roughly chopped

1 stick of celery, trimmed and roughly chopped

1 large carrot, peeled and roughly chopped

¼ of a swede, peeled and roughly chopped

2 tbsp olive oil

250g shin of beef, cubed

1 tbsp plain flour

Salt and freshly ground black pepper

330ml your favourite beer

350ml vegetable stock or gravy

1 bay leaf

For the suet dumplings

65g plain flour

35g shredded suet

½ tsp baking powder

½ tsp salt

2-3 tbsp cold water

For the beef stew

Fry the onion, celery, carrot and swede in a large, lidded casserole dish with half the olive oil until just starting to colour, then remove from the pan.

Dust the cubes of beef in seasoned flour and fry in batches on a high heat in the remaining oil. Aim to get some good colour onto the meat. Some of the meat juices and flour will caramelise on the base of the pan but this will be dissolved into the sauce when you add the beer. As the meat browns, transfer it to a plate before adding the next batch.

When all the meat is seared, pour the beer into the casserole and allow it to reduce slightly while scraping the bottom of the pan to mix in all the stuck-on flavour.

Pour in the vegetable stock and stir well, return the beef to the casserole, add the bay leaf and bring the mixture to the boil. Reduce the heat until the mixture is simmering, then leave to simmer gently for 1 hour with the lid slightly ajar.

For the suet dumplings

Mix the flour, suet, baking powder and salt in a bowl until well combined. Add the water gradually, stirring the mixture with your fingers, until it comes together as a soft dough. Shape the dough into balls roughly the size of a plum.

When the stew has been simmering for an hour, season it again with salt and pepper, if necessary. Place the dumplings on top of the stew, cover the casserole with the lid, and cook for a further 15 to 20 minutes, or until the dumplings have proudly puffed up. Serve straight away with mashed potatoes and a green vegetable such as spinach or kale.

GUJARATI STYLE SPINACH, CHICKPEA, LENTIL & CASHEW NUT CURRY

In India, this type of curry would usually be eaten as a thali with rice, a dhal and a snack like a pakora or bread made from flours including wheat, corn, millet or sorghum. You'll get the best and most authentic flavours by toasting and grinding your own fresh spices.

Prep: 15 mins

Cook: 45 mins

Serves: 4

1 bay leaf

1 cinnamon stick

3 cardamom pods

3 whole cloves

1 tsp cumin seeds

5 tbsp vegetable oil

6 medium onions, finely diced

6 cloves of garlic

6cm root ginger

8 green chillies

½ tsp ground turmeric

1 tsp red chilli powder

1 tsp garam masala

2 tsp ground coriander

2 tsp salt

100g tinned chopped tomatoes

1 x 400g tin of chickpeas

1 x 400g tin of lentils

Large bag of spinach leaves, washed

Handful of fresh coriander, chopped

50g cashew nuts, lightly toasted

Heat a heavy frying pan on a medium heat and dry fry the whole spices. First add the bay leaf, cinnamon stick, cardamom pods and cloves. Leave them for 30 seconds before adding the cumin seeds then let them fry for 1 or 2 minutes. Cool slightly then tip into a spice grinder or pestle and mortar and grind into a powder.

Heat the vegetable oil in a large pan on a medium heat. Let it warm up for a couple of minutes before adding the onions, then stir and cook for about 15 to 20 minutes, until they are golden brown. If the onions start to stick in the pan, just add a splash of water. Towards the end of this time, add the toasted spice powder.

Blend the garlic, ginger and green chillies together in a food processor. Once the onions are golden brown in colour, add the garlic paste to the pan and stir. After 1 minute, add one tablespoon of water and let it cook away, then add the turmeric, red chilli powder, garam masala, ground coriander and salt. Stir everything together, then add another tablespoon of water and let it soak in.

Add the chopped tomatoes with three tablespoons of water, cover and cook for 4 minutes, stirring occasionally. Drain and rinse the chickpeas and lentils then tip them into the pan with 300ml of hot water. Cover and simmer over a low heat for 5 minutes.

Fold in the spinach and cook gently for 5 minutes, to allow the spinach to wilt down, then serve the curry with rice, garnishing with the chopped coriander and toasted cashew nuts.

CHAPTER SEVEN: ENTERTAINING

SLOW ROAST SHOULDER OF LAMB WITH A SPRING HERB SALSA VERDE

Lamb is arguably one of the easiest meats to source where you can be sure of its grass-fed provenance, and if you live close to a farming district it makes sense to seek out the local animals.

Prep: 15 mins
Cook: 4 hours 30 mins
Serves: 6

2kg lamb shoulder

Olive oil

Salt and pepper

A few sprigs of fresh rosemary

2 onions, roughly chopped

2 carrots, roughly chopped

Several cloves of garlic (optional)

1 tbsp plain flour

Glug of red wine

1 stock cube or some vegetable stock

For the salsa verde

A bowl of foraged and perennial spring greens, such as wild garlic, dandelion, smooth sow thistle, rocket, cress and kale

8 tbsp olive oil

1 large dessertspoon Dijon mustard

A splash of cider vinegar

A few capers and gherkins

Salt and pepper

Score the fat on the lamb then rub the shoulder with olive oil and seasoning. Press the rosemary on top. Place the chopped onions, carrots and garlic in a roasting tin and lay the lamb shoulder on top. Cover the tin tightly with foil and place into a very hot oven. Turn the temperature down to 170°c and cook for 4 hours until the meat falls apart.

To make the salse verde in the meantime, simply blend all the ingredients together n a food processor and taste before adding more of your preferred flavours as needed.

Take the lamb out of the tray and wrap in foil to keep warm. Drain off most of the fat from the roasting tin and stir in the flour. Pour in some red wine and put the tin on the heat, using a wooden spoon to scrape the stuck-on goodness from the tray.

Let the wine reduce a little, then add enough stock – either a stock cube and boiling water or some reheated vegetable stock – to make a sauce.

Simmer until you achieve the consistency you like then pass through a sieve into a warmed jug. Serve the lamb, either sliced or pulled apart, with the salsa verde on the side.

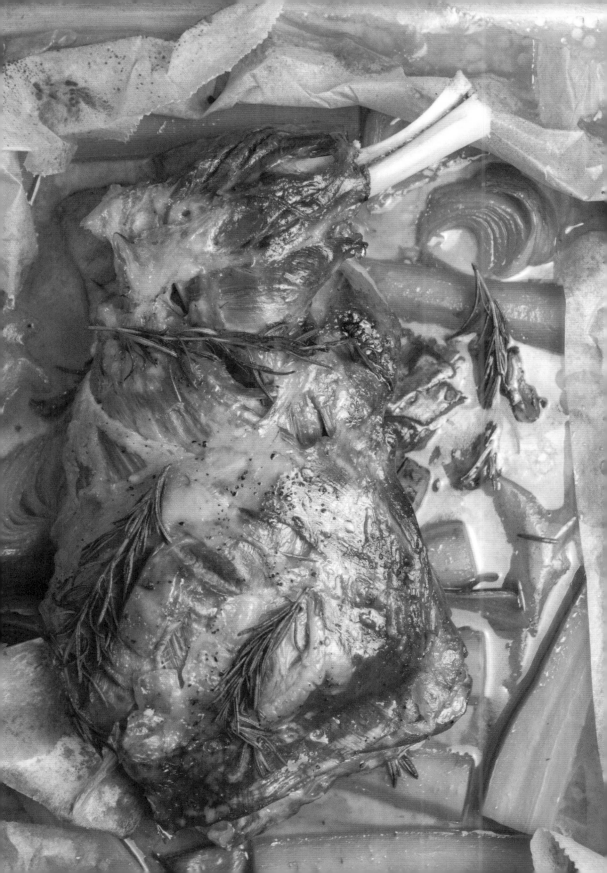

POTATO FONDANTS

These are simply potatoes cooked in a herby, buttery sauce. Fondants can be made the day before and then reheated to serve alongside a hearty dinner party dish. They go well with the Shin of Beef on page 96 or the Slow Roast Shoulder of Lamb on page 102.

Prep: 5 mins
Cook: 35-40 mins
Serves: 6

6 large potatoes (Maris Pipers are good)

1 tbsp olive oil

4 cloves of garlic, crushed

2 sprigs each of rosemary and thyme

150g unsalted butter

200ml vegetable stock

Peel the potatoes, then trim them to make the long sides flatter and the ends rounded, so you have evenly-sized oval 'boats'. Seal the potatoes in a hot frying pan (ideally one which can go into the oven) with the olive oil to get some colour on all sides.

After 5 or 6 minutes, season the potatoes, add the garlic to the pan and break in the herb sprigs. Add the butter to the pan, basting each potato boat once it has melted. Finally, pour in enough stock to come at least halfway up the potatoes.

Cover the pan with a lid or tin foil and transfer to the oven. Cook the fondants at 180°c until the potato is tender. Be careful not to overcook, as they will lose their shape and become difficult to handle. Serve straight away or cool for reheating later. In this case, it can be useful to undercook the potato slightly.

PEA PANNA COTTA

A delicate dish ideally made with new season peas, although frozen peas work equally well. Agar agar is made from red algae and is a great plant-based substitute for gelatine. You can make this into a really pretty starter by decorating with fresh herbs and edible flowers.

Prep: 20 mins

Cook: 5 mins

Serves: 4

300g peas

100ml milk

400ml double cream

2g powdered agar agar or powdered gelatine

Sea salt and white pepper

You could make this the day before for a stress-free dinner party, as it will be fine in the fridge overnight.

Blanch the peas for 1 or 2 minutes in boiling water then drain. Purée the peas with a stick blender or in a food processor. You may find it helps to add a little vegetable stock to break down the peas. Once blitzed, pass through a sieve to get a smooth purée.

Next, bring the milk and cream just to a boil and add the powdered agar agar or gelatine. Agar agar takes 1 or 2 minutes to completely dissolve so gently heat and whisk to ensure it is completely incorporated. Stir in the pea purée and check the seasoning, adding salt and white pepper to taste.

Pour the panna cotta mixture into four moulds; you can use individual dariole moulds, ramekins or shaped silicone moulds which can be easiest to turn out. Leave them in the refrigerator to set for a minimum of 3 hours, or overnight.

To serve, run a little hot water around the outside of the moulds and carefully turn out the panna cotta onto your plate. Decorate with fresh herbs and edible flowers.

ROAST COD WITH SHIITAKE MUSHROOMS & MISO BROTH

Cod is a robust fish which can stand up to the strength of the Asian seasonings. Nori provides a good source of niacin, which is present in many natural foods but its availability to the body can depend on how the ingredient is processed.

Prep: 15 mins
Cook: approx. 30 mins
Serves: 4

400g shiitake mushrooms

2 cloves of garlic or 1 tsp garlic paste

1 large onion, diced

Olive oil

4 sprigs of rosemary

Salt and black pepper

4 x 150-170g cod loin steaks

50g butter

For the broth

150ml fish stock

4 tsp miso paste

2 tsp sherry vinegar

To serve

300g brown or mixed brown and wild rice

2 sheets of nori (optional)

Fry the shiitake mushrooms, garlic and onion in some olive oil with the rosemary and some seasoning. Transfer them into a roasting tin lined with a large square of tin foil and place the cod steaks on top. Season the fish and dot the butter around the tin. Add a little of the fish stock and fold the tin foil over the top to form a parcel.

Cook the parcel in the oven at 180°c for 15 to 20 minutes, until the fish just turns translucent and is hot in the middle. Cook your rice at the same time according to the packet instructions.

Meanwhile, make the broth by heating the remaining fish stock with the miso paste and sherry vinegar. Once the fish is cooked, drain any liquid from the foil parcel into the broth. Pass it through a sieve to remove any little bits and keep warm in the pan.

Serve the fish and shiitake mushrooms on a bed of the cooked rice with the broth poured into the bowl. If you like, garnish the dish with nori, cut into strips and heated briefly in the broth.

SPINACH, SUN-DRIED TOMATO & RICOTTA ROULADE

This great meat-free dish can be the centrepiece of a family feast served alongside dishes such as the Multi Grain and Sprouting Seed Salad (page 44) and Sweet Potato Falafels (page 60).

Prep: 15 mins
Cook: 45 mins
Serves: 4

50g butter

40g plain flour, sifted

1 tsp Dijon mustard

200ml milk, warmed

50g mature cheddar cheese, grated

4 medium eggs, separated

3 tsp chopped mixed herbs

Salt and pepper

1 clove of garlic, peeled and crushed

1 medium leek, trimmed and finely sliced

225g frozen spinach, thawed and drained

¼ tsp freshly grated nutmeg

25g sun-dried tomatoes, drained and finely chopped

175g ricotta cheese

3 tsp freshly squeezed lemon juice

To garnish

15g sun-dried tomatoes, drained and cut into small, even pieces

1 sprig of fresh parsley

3 tsp freshly grated parmesan cheese

Preheat the oven to 200°c. Lightly grease a 23 by 33cm Swiss roll tin then line with baking parchment.

Melt half of the butter (25g) in a saucepan. Stir in the flour and cook the paste for 1 minute, then stir in the mustard. Gradually add the warmed milk to the pan, stirring constantly. Once it's all incorporated, bring the sauce to the boil and simmer for 1 to 2 minutes until thickened. Remove from the heat and leave to cool slightly.

Stir the cheese, egg yolks, mixed herbs and seasoning into the sauce. Whisk the egg whites in a clean bowl until stiff but not dry. Using a large metal spoon, carefully fold them into the sauce.

Spoon the mixture into the prepared Swiss roll tin and smooth out the surface. Cook in the oven for 10 to 15 minutes or until risen and golden.

Meanwhile, melt the remaining butter in a saucepan. Sauté the garlic and leek together in the butter for 3 minutes or until softened. Add the spinach with the nutmeg and cook for 5 minutes, then stir in the sun-dried tomatoes. Season to taste and set aside.

In a bowl, beat the ricotta and lemon juice together with seasoning to taste. Carefully turn the cooked roulade out of the tin and remove the lining paper. Carefully spread it with the ricotta and then the spinach and tomato mixture.

Roll up the roulade like a Swiss roll, starting from the short side. Transfer the roll to a baking tray and return it to the oven for 15 minutes, or until piping hot.

Garnish the baked roulade with the extra sun-dried tomatoes, fresh parsley and a sprinkling of parmesan. Cut into slices and serve immediately.

CELERIAC & CHESTNUT PIE WITH MUSHROOM SAUCE

Celeriac is an under-used vegetable with an earthy, nutty taste. It makes a great cold side dish grated and mixed with a combination of mayonnaise, Dijon mustard and lemon juice. This baked dish is an ideal autumnal supper.

Prep: 20-30 mins

Cook: approx. 1 hour

Serves: 6

400ml double cream

100ml whole milk

2 cloves of garlic, peeled and crushed

2 or 3 sprigs of fresh thyme

500g potatoes, peeled

500g celeriac, peeled

2-3 tbsp cornflour

2 tbsp olive oil

300g mixed fresh mushrooms (such as button, oyster, porcini)

100g cooked chestnuts

300g puff pastry

2 egg yolks, beaten with a little milk

Heat the cream and milk in a large saucepan with the garlic and thyme to infuse. Slice the potato and celeriac quite thinly (2-3mm): a mandoline is useful here, although a sharp knife can do just as well. Add the celeriac and potato to the saucepan and simmer for 5 to 7 minutes until the vegetables are starting to soften.

Drain and reserve the liquid. Mix the cornflour with a little of this to form a smooth paste. Pour the infused milk and cream back into the pan and thicken by stirring in the cornflour paste. Bring it back to a gentle simmer, then pass the sauce through a sieve and set aside.

In a separate pan, heat the oil while you slice the mushrooms. Fry them in the oil, increasing the heat as the water comes out of the mushrooms to give them a little colour. As they start to dry out, take the pan off the heat.

Butter or oil a pie dish and layer half the potato and celeriac in the bottom. Add a layer of the mushrooms and cooked chestnuts then a final layer of celeriac and potato. Preheat the oven to 200°c and leave the pie filling to cool while you roll out the pastry.

Cut out a lid from the puff pastry a little larger than your dish, and brush the rim of the dish with a little of the egg wash. Use strips of excess pastry to line the rim of the dish and form a border to stick the lid to. Lay the pastry lid over the dish and press down around the edges with your fingers to form a good seal. Make a couple of slits in the centre to allow steam to escape while cooking, and if you like add some decoration on top using leftover pastry cuttings.

Brush the whole pie thoroughly with the egg wash to ensure a good glaze. Bake in the preheated oven for 30 to 40 minutes until the pastry has risen, the filling is piping hot and the whole lid is golden brown. Serve with the reheated mushroom sauce on the side.

FREEKEH & BLACK BEAN STUFFED PEPPERS WITH SWEETCORN RELISH

These stuffed peppers have a real southern American feel thanks to the black beans and spicy sweetcorn relish. Freekeh has a slightly smoky flavour which goes very well with the barbecue vibe, and you could cook the peppers over hot coals in the summer.

Prep: 15 mins

Cook: 15 mins

Serves: 4

For the sweetcorn relish

200g sweetcorn

2 tomatoes, finely chopped

2 red chillies, chopped

1 small white onion, 2 baby onions or 2-3 spring onions, finely diced

½ a red pepper, diced

½ a green pepper, diced

25ml olive oil

25ml white wine vinegar

Small bunch of coriander, finely chopped

Salt and pepper

For the stuffed peppers

150g cracked freekeh

2 green peppers

2 red peppers

Olive oil

1 red onion, diced

3 cloves of garlic

1 tsp chilli powder

1 tsp oregano

½ tsp ground cumin

½ tsp cayenne pepper

1 x 400g tin of black beans, drained

For the sweetcorn relish

This is great made with fresh corn cut straight from the cob, but tinned or frozen sweetcorn is fine. For the tomatoes, it's best to only use the flesh here and put the watery/seedy part into the filling. Combine all the ingredients and leave in the fridge for the flavours to mingle.

For the stuffed peppers

Cook the freekeh in a saucepan with 300ml of water. It should take about 15 minutes, after which you can fluff it up with a fork. Be careful not to boil the pan dry, adding a little more water if required.

Leaving the stalks on, slice the peppers in half and remove the seeds. Brush inside and out with olive oil then season. Cook the peppers in the oven at 200°c for 15 minutes until soft and starting to very slightly colour. Keep them warm while you make the filling.

Fry the onion for 6 or 7 minutes until softened, then finely chop the garlic and add it to the pan with the chilli, oregano, cumin and cayenne. Cook for another 2 to 3 minutes then stir in the cooked freekeh, the watery parts of the tomatoes and the black beans. Cook for 5 minutes and then taste to check the seasoning.

Spoon the freekeh and black bean mixture into the pepper halves. Serve immediately with the sweetcorn relish on the side, or leave to cool and then refrigerate until needed. Reheat in the oven at 170°c for 15 to 20 minutes, perhaps with some grated cheese sprinkled over the top.

TOMATO & BARLEY RISOTTO

This is even better made with homegrown UK tomatoes in late summer when they have the best flavour. Alternatively, use tomato passata (see page 148) made when tomatoes are in plentiful supply and frozen in batches.

Prep: 5 mins

Cook: 40 mins

Serves: 4

1 tbsp olive oil

1 onion, finely diced

1 tsp garlic purée or 2 cloves of garlic, peeled and crushed

300g pearl barley

400ml tomato passata (see page 148 to make your own)

600ml vegetable stock

2 tsp dried oregano

1 x 400g tin of cannellini beans

100g pitted green olives

Salt and pepper

Basil leaves

Tomato crisps (see page 137)

Heat the oil in a pan then fry the onion and garlic until softened. Add the barley and stir for a couple of minutes to coat the grains in oil.

Add the passata and stock along with the oregano and simmer for 30 minutes or until most of the stock has been absorbed. The barley should still be just chewy. Add the cannellini beans and olives for the last 5 minutes and season to taste.

Divide the risotto between wide bowls, garnish with the basil leaves and scatter with dried tomato crisps.

JERUSALEM ARTICHOKE SOUP

This soup can be presented beautifully with the addition of a good quality truffle oil and some homemade vegetable crisps from the Store Cupboard chapter (see page 137).

Prep: 15 mins

Cook: 30-40 mins

Serves: 4

50g unsalted butter

2 tbsp olive oil

1 onion, finely chopped

2 sticks of celery, finely chopped

1 tsp garlic purée or 2 cloves of garlic, peeled and crushed

700g Jerusalem artichoke, cleaned, peeled and cut into chunks

150ml white wine

750ml vegetable stock

150ml double cream (optional)

Sea salt and white pepper

To garnish

Truffle oil

Vegetable crisps (see page 137)

Sprigs of chervil, sweet cicely or parsley

A note on the ingredients: Jerusalem artichokes are a knobbly tuber produced by the perennial plant and generally not ready in the UK until early autumn. They are a member of the sunflower family and are a good crop to grow if you have a large enough space, as once established they will tend to come back every year. One drawback of the tubers is that they contain a fair amount of inulin which is an indigestible starch. Leaving them in the ground into the winter and beyond helps as the plant naturally breaks this down into sugars, which as well as sweetening the crop makes it more digestible.

Melt the butter in the olive oil and gently fry the onion, celery and garlic until softened. Add the artichoke chunks and stir well to coat the vegetables in the fat. Pour in the white wine and allow the liquid to reduce by half. Add the vegetable stock and cook at a low simmer until the artichoke is tender and cooked through.

Blitz the soup with a stick blender or in a food processor, then season with sea salt and white pepper. For a super smooth finish, pass the soup through a fine sieve and for optional extra indulgence, swirl in the double cream.

To serve, ladle the soup into bowls and garnish with a drizzle of truffle oil, some vegetable crisps and a few delicate herb sprigs.

CHAPTER EIGHT: DESSERTS

BAKED CHOCOLATE & BEETROOT CHEESECAKE

Beetroot adds a sweet, earthy note to this decadent dessert. Using ricotta results in a lighter cheesecake mixture that still has a lovely creamy texture.

Prep: 25 mins

Cook: 35 mins

Serves: 6-8

For the base

200g Spelt Digestives or Almond Butter Biscuits (see page 58 and 48)

75g melted butter

For the filling

2 eggs

65g butter

65g caster sugar

135g ricotta cheese

1 large cooked beetroot

80g self-raising flour

20g cocoa powder

1 tsp baking powder or bicarbonate of soda

For the base

Crush the biscuits in a food processor, then combine with the melted butter and press into a 20cm springform cake tin. Chill until needed.

For the filling

Preheat the oven to 160°c. Separate the eggs, keeping both the yolks and whites. Beat the butter and sugar together until fluffy with a handheld electric whisk or in a stand mixer.

Beat the egg yolks into the creamed butter and sugar, then do the same with the ricotta until the mixture is smooth and silky. Grate the cooked beetroot into the bowl and fold in.

Whisk the egg whites in a separate bowl until stiff, then gently fold them into the beetroot mixture. Sift the flour, cocoa powder and raising agent together into the bowl and gently fold in so everything is incorporated.

Spoon the filling into the tin on top of the prepared base. Bake for about 35 minutes, until the middle of the cheesecake is slightly springy to the touch. Allow to cool in the tin for as long as it takes (about 1 hour) and don't worry if it sinks in the middle. Serve the baked cheesecake with whipped cream or ice cream.

CHOCOLATE & CHIA MOUSSE

This quick vegan dessert is delicious as well as really healthy. You can play with the level of sweetness versus bitterness from the cocoa powder with your chosen sweeteners.

Prep: 15 mins

Serves: 2-4

400ml coconut milk
(or another plant-based
alternative, like almond or
hazelnut milk)

60g chia seeds

50-70g cocoa powder

50ml maple syrup, or stevia
to taste

1 tsp vanilla extract

Put all the ingredients into a blender, starting with the lower amount of cocoa powder so you can add more to taste if needed. Blend the mixture until smooth then check the balance of sweetness to bitterness, adding more cocoa or syrup as needed.

When you're happy with the flavour, pour the mousse into glasses or ramekins. It will thicken up as the chia seeds absorb the liquid over about 10 minutes in the fridge.

There are endless flavour variations for this pudding. Try omitting the cocoa powder and vanilla, instead adding a cup of strawberries, or adding cinnamon and nutmeg for a chai chia mousse.

ROASTED STRAWBERRY & WHITE CHOCOLATE ICE CREAM

This easy ice cream is made extra delicious by first roasting the strawberries to intensify their flavour. Balsamic vinegar adds a sweet and sour depth, and the fat content of the coconut milk ensures that the resulting ice cream is soft and smooth.

Prep: 20 mins, plus churning or freezing

Cook: 20 mins

Serves: 4

200g fresh strawberries

1 tbsp balsamic vinegar

1 x 400g tin of full-fat coconut milk

3 tbsp coconut oil

3 tbsp maple syrup

2 tsp vanilla extract

100g white chocolate chips

Hull and roughly chop the strawberries, then spread them out on a parchment-lined baking tray and drizzle with the balsamic vinegar. Roast them in the oven for 20 minutes at 180°c. Remove and leave to cool.

To make the ice cream, tip most of the roasted strawberries into a blender along with all the other ingredients except the chocolate chips. Blend until smooth, then fold in the remaining strawberries and the chocolate chips. This gives the ice cream some texture.

Either use an ice cream machine according to the manufacturer's instructions, or pour the mixture into a lidded container and place into the freezer. Every hour or so, give the ice cream a good stir with a fork to break up larger ice crystals and make the mixture as smooth as possible. Do this three or four times, then leave to set completely.

It's best to take the container out of the freezer 15 minutes before serving, to allow the ice cream to soften before scooping into bowls or cones.

DAIRY-FREE & GLUTEN-FREE CHOCOLATE BROWNIE

Delicious and simple to make, this dessert is always a winner. It's especially indulgent reheated and served warm with ice cream for a special occasion!

Prep: 10 mins
Cook: 25-30 mins
Makes about 20

280g vegan dark chocolate

200g Flora or similar dairy-free spread

3 eggs or 150ml pasteurised liquid egg

200g brown sugar

100g gluten-free self-raising flour

Melt the chocolate and dairy-free spread in a metal bowl over a pan of barely simmering water. Whisk the eggs with the brown sugar in another bowl. When the chocolate mixture has melted, give it a whisk then pour it gradually into the egg mixture, still whisking, to combine the two.

Fold in the self-raising flour then pour the brownie batter into a 20 by 30cm tin lined with baking parchment. Bake at 160°c for approximately 20 to 25 minutes until the centre is only just set. You want the brownie to have a lovely gooey centre, as it will continue to firm up while it cools.

Leave the brownie to cool completely in the tin, then lift out and cut into small squares to serve.

BILBERRY FRANGIPANE TART

In hilly and moorland parts of the UK, it's always been a late summer tradition to pick bilberries. This can be a labour of love, but their rarity and unique flavour are worth the effort! If you can't get bilberries, UK-grown blueberries would work just as well.

Prep: 30 mins

Cook: 45-55 mins

Serves: 6-8

Hazelnut Shortcrust Pastry (see page 144)

150g butter

140g caster sugar

2 large free-range eggs

1 egg yolk

¼ tsp almond essence

Pinch of sea salt

150g ground almonds

30g plain flour

600g bilberries, picked over to remove stray stalks and washed

Preheat the oven to 180°c. Roll out the pastry to a circle a little larger than a 25cm loose-bottomed tart tin. Use this to line the tin carefully without stretching the pastry. Once in the tin and trimmed, rest in the fridge for at least 30 minutes.

Next, the pastry will need blind baking to prevent it becoming soggy. Crumple a piece of greaseproof paper or baking parchment then smooth out and tuck it gently over the pastry (crumpling the paper makes it easier to fit into the tin).

Fill the covered pastry case with loose pulses such as dried chickpeas, which will help keep the base flat. Bake in the preheated oven for 10 minutes, then remove the paper and pulses and cook for another 5 minutes. Remove the pastry case and turn the oven temperature down to 170°c.

Whilst the pastry case is baking, make the frangipane. Cream the butter and sugar together in a bowl with a hand whisk or using a stand mixer until there are no grainy particles left. Beat the whole eggs and egg yolk with the almond essence and salt, then gradually add this mixture to the creamed butter and sugar, a little at a time to prevent the mixture from splitting. When this is done, fold in the ground almonds and flour.

Fill the pastry case with the bilberries then carefully spread the frangipane over the top. You can make the frangipane layer a little thinner around the edges, as the mixture will spread in the oven and this can prevent it boiling over the side.

Bake the tart in the oven for 30 to 40 minutes until the frangipane is set and you can see the juice from the berries bubbling through. It can be useful to cover the tart with foil for the last 15 minutes if the top is browning too much.

Serve warm with crème fraîche or ice cream, or this tart is equally good served cold.

LEMON POSSET

One of the simplest but tastiest desserts to make. Ideal for special occasions as it can be made the day before and poured into your favourite glasses ready to set overnight in the fridge. Garnish with fruit, edible flowers or chocolate shavings just before serving.

Prep: 15 mins, plus 3 hours setting

Cook: 5 mins

Serves: 6

600ml double cream

200g caster sugar

2 lemons, zested

75ml lemon juice

This amount fills six 150ml wine glasses. Place the double cream and sugar along with the lemon zest into a large pan over a low heat. Slowly bring to the boil, cook for 3 minutes, then remove from the heat and allow to cool.

Add the lemon juice to the cream mixture and whisk well. Pour the posset into your serving glasses and refrigerate for a minimum of 3 hours or overnight. Garnish with fruit, edible flowers or chocolate shavings just before serving.

CHAPTER NINE:
STORE CUPBOARD

HOMEMADE STORE CUPBOARD & PRESERVING BUILDING BLOCKS

Cooking more sustainably can be easily kick-started by weaving certain habits and practices into your kitchen management, and trying not to rely on the supermarket for every last ingredient. By doing a little home growing or perhaps some local foraging and preservation, a store cupboard of essential ingredients can be quickly built up. Here are some ideas for minimising waste and making the most of seasonal harvests.

DEHYDRATOR MAGIC

Why magic? Well, because a simple and inexpensive home dehydrator can turn surplus food into delicious ingredients ready to fight another day! It's a brilliant way to reduce wastage by drying leftover bread, making delicious vegetable crisps, preserving overripe bananas to make amazing caramel-flavoured dried banana chips, and making perfect fruit leather. The manufacturer of the various models will give general guidance on times and temperatures depending on the type of food you are putting in the dehydrator, but even if you don't have this piece of equipment, a normal oven on its lowest temperature setting can usually be used to achieve the same results.

BREADCRUMBS

Bread is one of the most wasted foods in the UK, with an estimated 1.2 billion crusts binned each year. Save yours and when loading your dehydrator use the lower shelves to rack up the bread (this stops crumbs falling onto more delicate items like fruit and herbs). Once dried, they can simply be crumbled by hand, or whizzed in a food processor for a finer result. Store dried breadcrumbs in an airtight container for up to 6 months.

VEGETABLE CRISPS

Cut your choice of vegetables into slices approximately 4mm thick. Courgettes, carrots, squash, beetroot and parsnip are good, but you can use whatever is in season or that you need to use up. The slices can go straight into the dehydrator, or you can first toss them with a little olive oil and dried herbs or spices to give extra layers of flavour. Try rosemary and thyme, chilli and smoked paprika, orange zest and fennel, or ground cumin and sea salt. This also works with tomatoes, which you can simply slice and dehydrate to create the crisps used to garnish the Tomato and Barley Risotto on page 116. You may even want to dehydrate washed vegetable peelings, which can be stored in an airtight container and used to make an infused vegetable stock for soups and risottos.

BANANA, APPLE AND OTHER FRUIT CHIPS

Fruit such as apples, bananas and strawberries can be cut into 3 to 4mm slices and simply dried in a dehydrator according to the manufacturer's guidelines to create fruit chips. Sprinkling the apples with some cinnamon enhances their flavour. Dehydrating berries with skins is slightly different, as the skins need to be burst to ensure the fruit is dried. The easiest method is to freeze then plunge the berries into boiling water before draining and dehydrating. In this way, berries such as blackcurrants, redcurrants, bilberries and gooseberries can be made into your own mixed fruit selection. The freezing step is useful too, as it means you can harvest over a longer period as different fruits ripen, ready for a complete preservation session.

FRUIT LEATHER

Fruit leathers make a brilliant alternative to commercial fruit-flavoured sweets without the additives, and with all the natural flavour and nutrition intact. They can also look impressive as decorative scrolls or ribbons on desserts, and have a shelf life of at least 6 months at ambient temperatures.

Fruit leathers tend to look most impressive with darker fruits such as blackberries, raspberries and currants, although they are good with cubed apples added into the mix. Cook your chosen fruit mixture down with a little sugar, then when it has broken down and become very smooth, press the mixture through a sieve. Ideally, spread the fruit purée onto a reusable silicone baking mat (you could use baking parchment instead) and dehydrate until the 'leather' can be peeled off the mat or parchment and cut into strips or other shapes as desired.

GROW YOUR OWN

There is no better way to minimise food miles than to grow produce in your garden or even on your windowsill. The quickest harvests can be within 3 to 10 days, from sprouting seeds and growing pea and corn shoots.

SPROUTING SEEDS

All you need is an old wide-mouthed jam jar or re-used plastic tub and some seeds, such as alfalfa, radish or broccoli. Alternatively, it's very economical to use shop-bought dried legumes such as chickpeas, mung beans, green and brown lentils and aduki beans. Some of these may germinate more readily than others, depending on how well they have been kept and their age, so it's worth trying a small batch before buying a large amount.

To sprout your seeds or legumes, first soak a small handful overnight in your jar or tub. Remember that you will end up with a much bigger volume of sprouts than your original seeds, so be careful with the amount you use. The next day, carefully drain the seeds and leave them in the jar somewhere in your kitchen out of direct sunlight. Twice a day, rinse and drain the seeds. Within 3 days the seeds will start sprouting and may be ready to eat; you can experiment with the flavours over the next few days, as some sprouted seeds tend to become more bitter the longer you leave them. When they have sprouted, you can move the jar into direct sunlight which will tend to make them go a little greener. At this stage, simply rinse and they are ready to eat. You can also store the seeds in the fridge for up to 1 week, where they will still slowly grow and only need rinsing once a day.

GROWING PEA AND CORN SHOOTS

With a little more space, you can inexpensively produce these shoots using popcorn kernels and marrowfat peas. Fill a seed tray with peat-free compost and add a thick layer of the seeds, then cover them with a little more compost. Put the tray in a warm place such as a conservatory or greenhouse over the summer, or you could use a covered seed germination tray which has a small built-in heater during the winter. Give the planted seeds a good water and keep the soil moist for the next 7 to 10 days as the shoots develop and reach 10 to 15cm tall. To harvest the shoots, snip off the quantity you require, rinse and use in your recipe.

FORAGING

Foraging for our food was once a way of life for us all, with knowledge of the safest, tastiest and most nutritious plants and fungi passed down through the generations. As a result, our ancestors ate a much greater diversity of foods, perhaps over 100 plant varieties against generally less than 20 today (and these tend to be the high starch varieties). They would have supplemented these with wild meat, eggs, honey and fish, and studies show that the average height of European people before the onset of agriculture was up to 15cm taller than today, probably largely influenced by the quality of childhood nutrition.

Getting back to your roots is not only a hugely enjoyable way to experience the great outdoors but done safely it can also be a brilliant nutrition boost for our diets. Even in urban areas, there are generally green spaces, municipal plantings and parks which can provide your hunting grounds. Wild apple trees, for example, are common along the lines of disused railway tracks, probably thanks to apple cores thrown from train windows many years ago.

A TOP TEN OF UK WILD HARVESTS

PRODUCE	SEASON	USES
Nettles (the stinging variety or white/dead nettles)	Year round but best in the spring before they flower and when the younger nettle tops are most tender	Brilliant for nettle and potato soup, tempura, herbal tea
Sorrel, Dandelion, Smooth Sow Thistle	Best in the spring	Spring vegetable dishes, steamed & dressed with olive oil & seasoning
Wild Garlic	April/May	Leaves for pesto, flower buds as alternatives to capers, garnish
Elderflowers	May	Cordial, elderflower 'champagne'
Cherry Plums	July/August	Jam, compote
Blackberries	July/August/September	Pies and crumbles, jams and jellies, cordials
Rosehips	September/October	Rosehip syrup
Crab Apples/Wild Apples	September/October/ November	Crab apple jelly, cider
Blackthorn/Sloe	October-December (if the birds have left any)	Sloe gin
Hazelnuts	October/November (before the squirrels get them)	Snacking, pastry, pesto made with hazelnuts & sorrel

There are some clear rules for safe foraging along with the application of sound common sense! Ideally, do it in your own garden (let areas go wild to encourage the useful 'weeds' such as nettles, dandelions, clovers and smooth sow thistle) but if this is not possible ensure you have the landowner's permission. The Wildlife and Countryside Act (1981) makes it permissible to pick the fruits, seeds, flowers and leaf stems of plants but not to uproot them, providing these plants are not on the list of highly threatened species or in certain locations such as Sites of Special Scientific Interest (SSSI).

Most importantly, do not pick anything unless you are 100% sure that it is edible for humans. There are some extremely poisonous plants and fungi in Britain, and ingesting these can lead at worst to death and at best to extremely unpleasant stomach upsets. There are excellent field guides available to help you make these crucial distinctions.

FORAGED HERBAL TEA

Wild herbal teas have been crafted for centuries by herbalists and drunk for their medicinal qualities. Rich in vitamins and minerals, they are said to boost the immune system, soothe pains and detoxify. There is a good range of possible ingredients to choose from depending on the season, including wild rose and raspberry leaves, yarrow, nettles, blackcurrant and redcurrant leaves, white and red clover, elderflowers, meadowsweet, gorse leaf sprouts, ground ivy, hawthorn leaf, heather flowers, and dandelions. A short time in the dehydrator followed by gently crushing them into 'tea leaves' turns the foraged herbs into dried tea which can be stored in an airtight container for a long period.

As with any herb, it's important to start drinking foraged teas in small amounts and see how you respond. If you have a medical condition, are pregnant, nursing, or on medication, be sure to consult your physician about possible interactions, contraindications, and dosing.

ROSEHIP SYRUP

This lovely, deep-flavoured syrup can be made in autumn from hedgerow harvests and used throughout the year. Drink diluted like a cordial, or drizzle into porridge, desserts or cocktails. High in vitamin A and C, rosehips were widely collected in the Second World War to make syrup for children.

Prep: 45 mins
Cook: 20-25 mins
Makes 1.5 litres

500g rosehips
650g sugar

Blend the rosehips in a food processor to break open the fruit. You may see the very fine hairs around the cores, but these will be removed later by straining the liquid.

Bring 800ml of water to the boil in a large saucepan and add the blended rosehips. Bring back to the boil, stir and then leave to infuse off the heat for 15 minutes.

Strain the infused liquid through a jam bag, or improvise with a tea towel briefly dipped in boiling water lining a sieve sat over a bowl. Leave the liquid to drip through for a few minutes.

Repeat this process with another 800ml of boiling water, adding the strained rosehip pulp to the boiling water, bringing it back to the boil and leaving for another 15 minutes before straining and adding to the first batch of infused liquid.

In all there should now be about 1 litre of juice. Bring this to the boil then add the sugar, stirring to dissolve all the grains. Bottle the syrup in sterilised containers and cap or cork immediately. The syrup will keep for up to 4 months in the fridge.

CHERRY PLUM COMPOTE

Cherry plums are native to south-east Europe and western Asia, but have naturalised in the UK. In late summer, the crops of smallish round plums vary in colour from deep purple to orange and yellow. They can be made into jams, compotes, sauces or just eaten straight off the tree!

Prep: 5 mins
Cook: 30 mins
Makes 2 x 400g jars

300ml boiling water

150g caster sugar

500g cherry plums, stones removed

2 cinnamon sticks

3-4 whole star anise

Unless the plums are very ripe, it can be slightly fiddly to remove the stones. One trick is to simmer them in water until well broken down and then push them through a coarse sieve. If the plums are very ripe, simply squeeze them in your hands over a bowl, pulling the stones out as you go. This recipe also works with the common varieties of plums you can find in shops.

Heat a large saucepan and pour in the boiling water. Add the sugar and let the mixture bubble for 30 seconds, then add the plum purée, cinnamon sticks and star anise. Simmer the compote for 8 to 10 minutes, stirring gently until it thickens, then leave to cool.

Transfer the cooled compote to a jar and store in the fridge for up to 10 days. It goes well with the Buckwheat Pancakes on page 26.

HAZELNUT SHORTCRUST PASTRY

A rich, sweet pastry for special occasions. It makes a brilliant base for the Bilberry Frangipane Tart on page 130.

Prep: 10 mins
Makes enough for 1 x 25cm tart tin

140g butter

100g caster sugar

225g plain flour

50g ground hazelnuts

1 egg, beaten

Cream the butter and sugar together by hand or in a food processor. Stir in the flour and ground hazelnuts then bring the pastry together with the beaten egg. Shape the pastry gently into a smooth ball using your hands. If a little more moisture is needed to create a smooth dough then add a tiny splash of cold water.

Rest the dough for at least 1 hour in the fridge before use. It can be useful to roll out the pastry between two sheets of greaseproof paper so there's no need for additional flour, which can change the texture, and to prevent the pastry sticking to your work surface or rolling pin.

LEMON CURD

Homemade lemon curd is perfect for filling cakes, layering up fruit fools and trifles, adding to sweet tarts and, of course, in lemon meringue pie. It's also lovely as an ice cream topping or just on toast!

Prep: 10 mins
Cook: 20-25 mins
Makes 2 x 340g jars

4 unwaxed lemons, zested and juiced

200g unrefined caster sugar

100g unsalted butter, cubed

3 free-range eggs, plus 1 free-range egg yolk

Put the lemon zest, lemon juice, sugar and butter into a heatproof bowl. Sit the bowl over a saucepan of gently simmering water, making sure the water is not touching the bottom of the bowl. Stir the mixture every now and again until all of the butter has melted.

Whisk the eggs and egg yolk together then pour through a sieve into the lemon mixture. Whisk until all of the ingredients are well combined, then leave to cook for 10 to 13 minutes, stirring every now and again, until the mixture is creamy and thick enough to coat the back of a spoon. If you have a probe thermometer, the overall temperature should not rise above 82°c (any hotter risks splitting the eggs).

Remove the lemon curd from the heat and set aside to cool, stirring occasionally. Once cooled, spoon the lemon curd into sterilised jars and seal. Keep in the fridge for up to 3 weeks until ready to use.

ALMOND BUTTER

This works anywhere you would use peanut butter, such as spread on toast or crackers for a snack, and is used to make delicious biscuits in the recipe on page 48.

Prep: 5-10 mins
Cook: 10 mins
Makes 1 x 300g jar

300g whole almonds, skins on

Drizzle of honey or coconut oil (optional)

For best results, roast the almonds in the oven at 190°c for 10 minutes. Allow them to cool and then blend in your food processor, stopping to scrape down the sides when necessary, until you have the right consistency. If you like, add a little honey for sweetness or coconut oil for a smoother texture. Transfer into a sterilised jar and keep in the fridge for up to 3 weeks.

MAYONNAISE

The prospect of making mayonnaise can be a little scary but it's well worth a go, as the end result is very satisfying and very tasty. It's important to use high quality free-range fresh eggs; look out for the British Lion stamp which shows they are from certified salmonella-free flocks.

Prep: 5 mins

Makes 300ml (enough for about 6 people)

1 tsp Dijon mustard

2 egg yolks

30ml white wine vinegar or lemon juice

250ml light vegetable oil (such as sunflower)

Put the mustard, egg yolks and vinegar or lemon juice into a large bowl. Whisk together then begin to slowly pour in the oil while still whisking vigorously. As the mixture starts to emulsify and thicken you can add the oil more rapidly. If you add the oil too quickly the mixture can split, but if this happens you can rescue the mayonnaise by starting again with the same ingredients and gradually whisking the split mixture into the new one.

The mayonnaise can get quite thick so can be let down with a little cold water, vinegar or lemon juice to taste. Serve straightaway or, as this contains raw egg, keep the mayonnaise for a maximum of 2 days in the fridge.

The flavour variations here are virtually endless. A brilliant Scandanavian touch, which is great with cured fish, is to fold through chopped fresh dill and a little more lemon juice. Adding garlic purée makes this very similar to Spanish aioli, and combining mayo with sweet chilli sauce makes a very quick and easy dressing for slaws and salads.

PASSATA

When made with your own or locally grown tomatoes, particularly when there is a late summer glut, the flavour will be immeasurably superior to any shop-bought passata. It's extremely versatile as a tomato sauce for pasta, in the risotto on page 116 or anywhere you would normally use tinned tomatoes.

Prep: 15 mins
Cook: 1 hour
Makes 2 x 500g jars

2kg ripe tomatoes

200g onions, diced

4 cloves of garlic

50ml olive oil

1 tsp salt

Freshly ground black pepper

Sprigs of rosemary, thyme, basil or oregano

Preheat the oven to 180°c. Roughly cut the tomatoes into chunks and arrange on a baking tray lined with baking parchment. Mix in the onions and garlic, drizzle over the oil and scatter with the salt, pepper and herb sprigs. Roast the tomatoes in the preheated oven for 1 hour. This evaporates the excess water and adds colour, concentrating the flavours.

Remove the tray from the oven and tip all the contents into a sieve over a clean container (with a lid) or a jug for decanting the passata into jars. Push as much of the roasted tomato as possible through the sieve into the container to get a lovely smooth sauce.

Either use the sauce immediately, keep for up to 3 days in the fridge or freeze for longer storage.

CARAMELISED ONIONS

These are a great base for soup or the tomato tart on page 34 as well as a flavour-packed addition to toasted sandwiches. They will keep for several days in the fridge.

Prep: 5 mins
Cook: 30 mins
Makes enough for 1 tart

4 onions, sliced

Splash of olive oil

2 tbsp Henderson's Relish

If you can't find Henderson's Relish (a vegan condiment made in Sheffield) then substitute with Lea & Perrins or Worcestershire sauce.

Slowly sweat down the sliced onions in a pan with a little olive oil, adding Henderson's Relish and seasoning to taste. The onions will gradually darken until sticky, dark brown and unctuous.

Cook for at least 30 minutes with a lid on the pan, stirring occasionally and adding a splash of water if they get too dry, until the onions are completely caramelised. Cool slightly before storing in an airtight container and refrigerating.

APPLE CHUTNEY

Chutneys are a great way to preserve gluts of local fruit and vegetables when harvests are plentiful in the autumn. There may even be trees in your neighbourhood whose fruits aren't being used, perhaps because they're a sour cooking variety like Bramleys, but these are perfect for chutney.

Prep: 5 mins, plus overnight
Cook: up to 2 hours
Makes 2 x 500g jars

1.5kg apples

2 onions

2 cloves of garlic

7.5cm ginger

1 tsp sea salt

400g raisins

700ml cider vinegar

750g muscovado sugar

The evening before you want to make the chutney, chop the apples, onions, garlic, and ginger. Sprinkle the chopped fruit and vegetables with the salt and leave them in the fridge overnight, allowing the salt to draw out some of the juices.

The next day, add the remaining ingredients to the salted fruit and vegetables in a large saucepan. Bring slowly to the boil then simmer for up to 2 hours, stirring well particularly towards the end as the chutney thickens.

The chutney will continue to thicken as it cools, so you need to judge the point when it's ready to bottle carefully. Transfer the chutney into sterilised jars and seal with the lids while the mixture is still very hot. A vacuum will form in the jar as the chutney cools, preserving it for up to a year.

WILD GARLIC PESTO

Wild garlic grows prolifically from March to May in shaded woodland areas on the damp margins of river beds and brooks. The flower buds can be picked and pickled, and this pesto can be stirred into pasta, used in savoury tarts or spread on good bread and grilled to make bruschetta.

Prep: 45 mins
Cook: 20-25 mins
Makes 2 x 400g jars

A small carrier bag of wild garlic leaves

300g olive oil

100g pine nuts

80g hard cheese, grated (parmesan works well)

Squeeze of lemon juice

Salt and pepper

First, wash the wild garlic well. Soak in cold water, then rinse and place in a colander to drain. Blend half of the wild garlic with the rest of the ingredients to taste in a food processor or using a stick blender. Add more wild garlic leaves until the consistency is similar to a thick purée, tasting to see if you need more salt, pepper or lemon juice to cut through the rich garlic flavour.

This pesto keeps well in the fridge for up to 2 weeks with a film of olive oil over the top to keep out the air. It also freezes well, which can be done in convenient portions so you can have the right quantities to hand for pasta dishes, tarts and bruschetta in the future. It's worth making large batches while you can, as the season is short and the crop prolific. If you can't get any wild garlic, this recipe works with a large bunch of basil instead.

BASIC VINAIGRETTE

A vinaigrette is an emulsion of oil and acid flavoured with mustard, herbs or spices. The starting point is one quarter acid to three quarters oil, but you can vary these proportions according to your own taste.

Prep: 5 mins
Makes 1 x 400ml jar

300ml light rapeseed, sunflower or olive oil

100ml white wine or cider vinegar

2 tsp Dijon mustard

Sea salt and ground white or black pepper

Put all the ingredients into a screw top jar and shake vigorously. You can then serve the vinaigrette from this jar, re-shaking before use or decant into a more presentable jug for the table. Keep in the fridge for up to a week with the lid tightly sealed.

It's easy to vary the flavours of this basic vinaigrette by changing the type of oils and acids used. Try substituting the vinegar with lemon, orange or lime juice, using balsamic vinegar or adding additional flavours such as finely chopped shallots or garlic.

'QUICK' SOURDOUGH BREAD

Although there is no truly quick method for making sourdough, this recipe involves the smallest amount of prep and then a simple turn out and bake the following morning. You'll need two 1kg bannetons (a traditional bread basket for proving the dough) and a sourdough starter, which is a way of developing a 'wild' yeast culture from the naturally occurring yeasts within flour, as well as various beneficial lactic acid bacteria which give the resulting bread its pleasingly 'sour' edge.

Prep: 20 mins, plus overnight proving and 1 week for homemade starters

Cook: 40-50 mins

Makes 2 large loaves

500g strong white bread flour (ideally, use a locally milled or organic flour to maximise the wild yeast content)

500g wholemeal or spelt flour

600ml water

250g sourdough starter

15-20g salt, to taste

To make the starter, begin 1 week in advance of baking. On Day 1, mix 50g of bread flour with 50ml of warm water in a ceramic bowl big enough to contain six more doses. Drape over a tea towel to prevent unwanted visitors but allow air exchange, and leave the bowl out in your warm kitchen. Every day for 5 or 6 days thereafter, add a further 50ml of warm water and 50g of flour. You should notice some activity in the form of bubbles and a pleasant beery, fruity and gassy smell. Once active, the starter will need using. If you're making bread daily it can be kept out of the fridge with the regime maintained. To slow down the activity, keep in the fridge and only feed every 3 days.

To make your sourdough, place all the ingredients in a large mixing bowl. By hand or using a stand mixer with a dough hook on a slow speed, mix together until all the water has been absorbed and the dough comes away from the sides of the bowl. It should look smooth, and will have required 7 or 8 minutes of kneading.

Turn your dough out onto a clean work surface and split in half. Working with one half at a time, knead in the edges to smooth out the dough again, turn upside down then turn quickly into a round. Very lightly dust the top with flour and then place topside down into your banneton. Ideally, place the basket into a large plastic bag, leaving space for the dough to rise, to create a humid environment. Leave the dough to prove overnight (12 hours or so) in a cool place (10 to 12°c) so that the fermentation can be slow and steady.

The next morning, preheat your oven to 220°c. Turn the proved dough out onto large baking trays, slash the top with a sharp knife or razor and bake for 6 to 8 minutes in the preheated oven, before turning the temperature down to 180°c. Bake for a further 30 to 40 minutes until the loaves are well coloured and the bottoms sound hollow when tapped. Once done, cool on a wire rack before slicing. The loaves freeze well once cooled.

ABOUT THE AUTHOR

Peter Taylor studied Nutritional Medicine (BSc) under Dr L Plaskett and, whilst practising in the West of England, wrote two books. *Overweight? Overtired? The Solution* and *What's In My Food?* were both written in response to the grave concern Peter has regarding the physical pain and misery many of his clients suffered due to poor food choices. Since that time, climate change has become the major challenge for humanity. Having read reports from The EAT-Lancet Commission and the Intergovernmental Panel on Climate Change (IPCC) during 2019, it became clear to Peter that food production and consumption has an enormous impact on the health of people and their planet. He found that making small adjustments to what we eat can collectively have a significant effect on the reduction of greenhouse gas emissions. It was this that persuaded Peter to create a book of recipes which can encourage those changes, alongside some stark facts from the reports to reinforce the need for more self-restraint in our food choices.

"Food is to be enjoyed. Without the joy of food, one might as well give up the will to live. But there is a difference between enjoying food and greed. With a little restraint, good food can be enjoyed because quality will always achieve more delight than quantity."

ABOUT THE CHEFS

PJ taste are Sheffield-based champions of seasonally inspired local food. Working sustainably has always been at the heart of the business and our flourishing forest garden produces everything from honey to soft fruit and perennial vegetables. We use this produce in our delivered catering for businesses and families in South Yorkshire and Derbyshire.

It's been a pleasure to contribute recipes to this book and share some of the methods we have developed over 15 years of business to produce food which is not only delicious but minimises the impact on the planet. This is a win-win game, as utilising what's in your store cupboard, buying seasonally and perhaps a little home growing and preserving is good for the pocket, as well as being nutritionally superior to relying on manufactured meals.

Special thanks to Chef Emily who helped me devise, check and cook these dishes through the very difficult summer of 2020.

Peter Moulam

WHAT DO WE DO AT MEZE PUBLISHING TO REDUCE OUR IMPACT ON CLIMATE CHANGE?

The Climate Change Cook Book

First edition printed in 2021 in the UK
by Bell and Bain Ltd, Glasgow
ISBN: 9781910863671
Written by: Peter Taylor and Katie Fisher
Designed by: Paul Cocker and Phil Turner
Recipes by: PJ taste
Photography by: Marc Barker
Contributors: Michael Johnson, Emma Toogood, Sarah Haworth
Published by: Meze Publishing Limited, Unit 1b, 2 Kelham Square,
Kelham Riverside, Sheffield S3 8SD
Web: www.mezepublishing.co.uk
Telephone: 0114 275 7709
Email: info@mezepublishing.co.uk

As you can see from the certification stamp on the back cover, the paper used in the production of this book is FSC certified. The Forest Stewardship Council certifies forests all over the world to ensure they meet the highest environmental and social standards. Products made with wood and paper from FSC forests are marked with the 'tick tree' logo. When you see this logo, you can be confident that buying that product won't mean harming the world's forests.

Our printers, Bell & Bain, are UK-based whereas many publishers use larger operations abroad. They have a longstanding commitment to a more environmentally friendly approach in the production of books and journals, with around 98% of all paper purchased by the company accredited with FSC® Chain of Custody Certification, and over 75% of all the printed matter they manufacture carries an FSC® Chain of Custody claim.

We distribute the majority of our products in-house, using warehouse facilities just a few minutes' drive from our office in Sheffield, as this helps to reduce the distance that our books travel from the printer to the customer. Much of the packaging we use in the warehouse - cardboard boxes, packing paper and bubble wrap (with the exception of envelopes and parcel tape) - is 'second hand' as we save and reuse all packaging from our printers and returns rather than purchasing new materials. This includes wooden pallets used for large shipments, and we are also switching to eco-friendly biodegradable pallet wrap to replace the standard plastic version.

Our main wholesaler, Gardners Books, have a 'green approach' that ensures they use recyclable, reusable and plastic-free boxes and wraps, with recycled or biodegradable packaging. For over a decade, they have run a 'zero waste to landfill' initiative, instead sending non-recyclable waste to an Energy Recovery Facility which sends heat to the National Grid. Along with reducing their warehouse lighting energy use and only using recyclable cups in their canteen, Gardners are demonstrably committed to reducing waste for a more environmentally friendly supply chain.

In our own office, we aim to make as many small but important choices as possible to reduce our carbon footprint. This includes having recycling facilities for everyday items; printing in black and white on recycled paper, or not at all where possible; switching to LED lightbulbs; having our electric heaters on timers; and buying eco-friendly loo roll from the brilliant B Corp, Who Gives A Crap. We often travelled within the country to meet with clients before the Covid-19 pandemic, but the UK's lockdown meant we had to move everything online. Since we saved time, energy and money by not having to travel, and by sharing digital rather than printed resources, we will be continuing to use video calling platforms for the vast majority of our internal and client meetings going forward.

Meze is a member of the Independent Publishers Guild (IPG) and within that organisation, we are part of the Sustainability Action Group who are working to reduce the environmental impact of publishing as an industry. The group's inception was shortly followed by the coronavirus pandemic and complete shutdown for many offices, but there is plenty of work to do as we get back on our feet, and in the longer term, for this group and its crucial goal.

BIBLIOGRAPHY

Reducing Food's Environmental Impacts through Producers and Consumers, J. Poore and T. Nemecek, Science, Volume 360, Number 6392, 2018

Food in the Anthropocene: the EAT–Lancet Commission on healthy diets from sustainable food systems, Willett, Walter et al., The Lancet, Volume 393, Issue 10170

Climate Change and Land: an IPCC special report on climate change, desertification, land degradation, sustainable land management, food security, and greenhouse gas fluxes in terrestrial ecosystems, P.R. Shukla, J. Skea, E. Calvo Buendia, V. Masson-Delmotte, H.- O. Pörtner, D. C. Roberts, P. Zhai, R. Slade, S. Connors, R. van Diemen, M. Ferrat, E. Haughey, S. Luz, S. Neogi, M. Pathak, J. Petzold, J. Portugal Pereira, P. Vyas, E. Huntley, K. Kissick, M. Belkacemi, J. Malley (eds.), IPCC, 2019

Greenhouse gas mitigation potentials in the livestock sector, M. Herrero, B. Henderson, P. Havlík et al., Nature Climate Change 6, 2016

The State of World Fisheries and Aquaculture 2018, Food and Agriculture Organisation of the United Nations (FAO)

Your Questions About Food and Climate Change, Answered, Julia Moskin, Brad Plumer, Rebecca Lieberman and Eden Weingart, The New York Times, 30th April 2019

www.leafuk.org

www.soilassociation.org/certification

www.msc.org/what-we-are-doing/our-approach/ what-does-the-blue-msc-label-mean

www.rspo.org

www.worldwildlife.org/pages/which-everyday-products-contain-palm-oil

www.rainforest-alliance.org/faqs/what-does-rainforest-alliance-certified-mean

www.terracycle.com/en-GB/about-terracycle

www.theguardian.com/environment/2020/jan/28/ what-plant-milk-should-i-drink-almond-killing-bees

ENDORSEMENTS

"We are pleased to endorse The Climate Change Cook Book because we share its commitment to making a difference, to both environmental sustainability and human health, through the food we eat and the way it is produced. The Institute for Sustainable Food is dedicated to understanding the complexities of the food system and to making system-wide change, applying the lessons of cutting-edge science to generate practical solutions to real-world problems. Our research shows that food systems are complex things and we should not underestimate the power of individuals, working alone, to make transformative changes through our dietary choices. We also need large-scale institutional change, led by governments, businesses and civil society organisations. But we cannot wait for others to make radical system-wide changes on our behalf, and this cook book invites us all to take some simple steps to improve our planetary and personal health. Based on sound science, the book makes a reasoned case for dietary change with a series of easy-to-follow, beautifully illustrated ideas for making tasty and nutritious meals. It is a recipe for change that we can all follow."

Professor Duncan Cameron and Professor Peter Jackson, Co-Directors of the Institute for Sustainable Food, University of Sheffield

"The Climate Change Cook Book gives readers a brilliant choice of sustainable recipes to help your immune system and tackle climate change. There are tasty recipes such as Buckwheat Pancakes and Baked Chocolate & Beetroot Cheesecake that even young children will enjoy."

Dr Mya-Rose Craig, Ornithologist & Climate Activist (www.birdgirluk.com)